FORTUNE IS IN THE FOLLOW-UP®

FIVE POWER STRATEGIES TO
REINVENT YOUR MARKETING

HEIDI BK SLOSS

The Fortune is in the Follow-Up®: FIVE Power Strategies to Reinvent Your Marketing
Second Edition
Heidi BK Sloss

Copyright© 2012
ISBN: 9780985266974
Library of Congress Control Number: 2012952272

Published by 3L Publishing
www.3LPublishing.com

ENDORSEMENTS

"Heidi Sloss sees business for exactly what it is: the treasures are in the follow-up, don't ignore customers after the purchase, and cultivate (long-lasting) relationships. This book reveals the crucial steps business owners must take to be profitable in any economy. Believe me, you'll really enjoy reading this book as much as earning a fortune from it!"
- Jay Conrad Levinson, The Father of Guerrilla Marketing, Author, *Guerrilla Marketing* series of books, over 21 million sold; now in 62 languages

"Growing your business can be simple, but it's not always easy. Heidi's book gets right to the heart of what every entrepreneur wants to know—what are the most effective and efficient business-building strategies, and how can I implement them quickly? *The Fortune is in the Follow-Up*® is practical, straightforward, and filled with easy-to-follow advice focused on taking action."
- C.J. Hayden, Author, *Get Clients Now!*™

"Simple, straightforward, and highly effective, this book demonstrates how making human connections in business makes all the difference."

- Marcia Conner, Social Business Industry Analyst and coauthor of *The New Social Learning*

"In *Fortune is in the Follow-Up*®, Heidi Sloss encourages readers to stick to business basics. By focusing on the things you can control, Heidi reveals tactics that deliver profitable and lasting business results, including happier clients, more closed sales, and overall higher satisfaction as business owners. Her timeless action items are just what you need in order to see profits this very year. Job well done!"

- Patrick Schwerdtfeger, Speaker and Author of *Marketing Shortcuts for the Self-Employed* (2011, Wiley)

DEDICATION

This book is dedicated to small business owners everywhere who have big dreams and little wallets. You are the engine of our future economy.

To my father, my original mentor and business partner.

And to my husband, David, and children, Kamala and Dakin, thank you for your support, understanding, and patience.

Transcriptions and a formal market survey template
are available at:

www.fortuneisinthefollowup.net/readers-special-gift

CONTENTS

INTRODUCTION

As a small Business Mentor, I see clients who have considerable skills and talents, but still struggle to grow their businesses. Some labor under the impression that without lots of capital, it is almost impossible to grow a successful business. This is not true. There are many options available to entrepreneurs to help them create successful profit centers from their businesses that do not involve huge influxes of capital. This book describes what I have learned from running several different businesses in many different industries and from my clients in my private business mentoring practice.

Too many business owners run around like chickens without their heads, racing from one networking event to the next, or jumping on the latest and greatest bandwagon for marketing and promoting their businesses, never gaining enough traction to successfully grow a viable business venture. Others have unrealistic timeframes of what it takes to grow a profitable business, and many who have sound business concepts, identifiable and viable target markets, and talent and creativity are still not making any money.

WHAT'S THE PROBLEM?

Simply put: Sound business principles are missing. In fact, I considered calling this book, *How to Grow Your Business in a Crappy Economy;* however, I realized that the strategies that I have used successfully to grow my own businesses and my clients' businesses are timeless—they work in times of expansion and times of contraction. And, while I don't like to always admit it, I have been around long enough to see the pendulum swing a few times. What was booming before, and might not be now, will boom again.

It's important for all business owners, whether large, small, or in between, to be proactive with current times. A great example of a proactive business strategy is companies that sell pool equipment in the summer and holiday decorations in the winter. They are following marketplace demands.

Unfortunately, gone are the days of "build it and they will come!" Now business owners must not only build it, but they must also search out new and emerging markets for their goods and services. In order to do so successfully, business owners must have the ability to think strategically and see the big picture.

Far too often, I work with talented business owners who know how to offer great goods or fabulous services, but they do not understand how to run a marketing and sales venture, which is a significant business misstep. To succeed in business today, business owners need to excel in marketing and sales. Period.

Also far too often, I read and hear all sorts of overly complicated business advice. In my work and in this book, I strive to provide easy-to-understand advice. My clients leave my programs or private sessions with bite-size action items that they can implement right away. This book presents concepts in the same fashion.

My hope is that most of what I present is not new to you. Ideally, you have heard this information (or information similar to it). My goal is that after reading it here, it will inspire you to stop reading, stop complaining, and start doing. Action is the name of the game. "Analysis paralysis," anxiety, and/or thinking about the solutions to business growth problems are real roadblocks for many business owners. To avoid these barriers, take the information and resources I offer and make the best decision you can to move forward—and make no mistake, moving forward is key for business growth and success.

One of my clients wanted to use eNewsletters as a way to communicate with her prospects and clients. She spent months trying to get the "perfect" drafts together for her newsletter campaign. She agonized over having her database up to date and used every excuse in the book to avoid sending out her eNewsletters. She missed out on six months of communicating with her prospects and clients. Instead of moving forward in her business, she was moving backward.

Another problem I have observed is business owners who don't properly use networking as a strategy in their marketing plans. They see the importance of attending networking events so they can find new clients; however, they rarely, if ever, follow-up with the people they have met. In fact, when I speak to groups of entrepreneurs and ask them what they do with the business cards they collect, the most common answer is that the cards are sitting on a shelf or in a drawer collecting dust—not effective, not productive, and definitely not revenue generating.

RUNNING A BUSINESS IS OVERWHELMING

The constant search for new people and new clients is draining. Too many business owners come to me with full calendars. They are overwhelmed and still not making money. All business owners must meet new people to be constantly priming their prospect pipelines. This is a key part of marketing. But when business owners lose sight of the reason for meeting new people—to build meaningful relationships with prospects until they want to do business with you—then the networking becomes a waste of time. Just adding contact information of new people you meet into your database without understanding what or why you are doing this is worthless.

Many business owners seek my advice, after having spent many hours and dollars going to events trying to meet prospects and referral sources. And if that initial meeting did not produce immediate results, they are onto the next event, meeting new people, rather than investing more in the relationships they just started.

5 POWER STRATEGIES

This book was written to explain how to REALLY grow a business using five power strategies:

- **Define Your Target Market,**
- **3 Secrets of Successful Delegation,**
- **Find the Fortune in Your Follow-Up,**
- **7 Stellar Customer Service Strategies and**
- **Why Mindset Matters**

Why five? Why not four or six? There's no particular reason, except that these five, plus the two bonus strategies on **How to Create a Marketing Plan** and **The Power of Networking**, are enough to set up a solid foundation for business growth for any business in any economy.

For the most part, I have tried to make sure that the information presented works for both service providers and product suppliers—although for some businesses, you may have to do some 'translations' in your head to apply the strategy to your particular business.

The five strategies I present have worked for me, my clients, and they will absolutely work for you. These are not the only ones, but they are great to get you going—or to revitalize you on your way. I am all about the "get you going!"

And I have included two bonus strategies: **How to Create a Marketing Plan** and **The Power of Networking: 5 Simple Strategies to Make Money.** Each Power strategy is presented in a separate chapter, and each chapter has action Items.

I use the word POWER very deliberately in this book to describe the five strategies that will grow your business and make you more money in the process. The root of the word "power" comes from the old French verb, *pooir*, which means to be able. I use the word in this context—with these five strategies and the two bonus ones, because these will help you have the ability to perform effectively, with strength, influence, and control over your business—the very definition of power these days.

When I think of a business owner, I think of people who are in control of their own financial destinies. Employing these POWER strategies will give you, as a business owner, the capacity to grow your business, achieve your dreams, and make more money. I have done it and so can you.

MY BACKGROUND AS A SERIAL ENTREPRENEUR

For many years, I have been told by different people that I should write a book, but the origins of this particular book began when we moved back to the San Francisco Bay Area in 2008 as the economy tanked. Moving a business across the country is never easy, much less during times of economic crisis. But this did not stop me, because I have a passion for helping business owners grow their businesses and achieve their dreams. I know what they need to do in order to create a profitable business on a limited budget, and I know what the barriers are for their success because I have been there and done that in many different businesses in multiple locations in this country.

My professional career has been one typical of many women in my generation—lots of transitions, constantly reinventing myself professionally, all while balancing the needs of my children and family. I could have written a book called *The Art of Successful Transitions for Women and Mothers*, but I will leave that to someone else.

The other possible title could have been *All I Learned in Business I Learned While Starting a Business with my Father*, because the first step of my professional life began while I was still in college in 1980. I decided to spend a year living in New York, working for my father's brand new business while writing my college thesis.

He had just started a company with an investor in the industry in which he had worked for almost two decades: men's accessories for the better men's specialty shops and department stores. My father designed and colored the line, ordered the fabric, and then contracted with local factories to sew together the neckties and other assorted menswear accessories. We were primarily private label manufacturers, which meant that we usually put the stores' labels on the neckties and other accessories, rather than our own.

He had lots of contacts from his many years in the industry working for another company, but needed to work those contacts in order to grow the new business. Meeting new people was important, of course, but it was his relationships with the buyers and vendors he already knew that made the difference in being able to launch and successfully grow our business without much capital.

Two of the first things I learned from my father were to cultivate who you know and always treat everyone well—you never know when you will want or need something from someone. (Remember the golden rule?) While there are almost 7 billion people on the planet, the world has a way of seeming small when you keep running into the same people in different industries. We grew the business with many of the same people he had met while working for other companies in the menswear world in the 1960's and 1970's.

After a few years of growing that company, we left his partner and started our own company in the same industry. We were business partners for 5 or 6 years, and I owe a huge debt of gratitude to my father for entrusting me with the roles he did when I was only in my early 20's.

In the first company, my first responsibility was bookkeeping, but that soon grew to include overseeing the employees, both in the manufacturing end and in the office. Eventually, I added sales to my responsibilities and even helped my father in coloring the line— although this was his talent and skill base.

During the nine years we worked together, I learned a tremendous amount of practical action items to grow a business with limited capital. Merchandising a clothing line, marketing with little or no budget, sales conversations with big and little (and in between) national and international stores, local and offshore manufacturing, importing, and exporting, shipping, and employee relations were just some of the many tasks that filled my days at that company. In some ways, I received a crash MBA and a family business degree all rolled up into one during my time in New York in the 1980's.

A key component to success in any business is to have a support system. My father was not only my parent during our partnership, he was also a key part of my support system. Additionally, I connected with some wonderful women through the University of Pennsylvania's Wharton Applied Research Center by participating in the then Women in Family Owned Business Program. Afterward, I was one of the founding members (and first president) of the now defunct Women in Family Owned Business Association (WIFOB). We met quarterly to learn and discuss the key challenges and opportunities of combining work and family life. Some of my fondest memories of that time are discussions with other women talking about the ins and outs of family business systems.

After leaving New York to get married in 1989, I took time off to figure out what inspired me. I had heard people talk about their professional careers as something they loved to do—that they were so motivated by what they were doing, they could not believe that they actually got paid for it. I wanted to feel that way but needed to figure out what that would be for me.

Over the next two decades, my husband and I moved a lot. We first lived in Washington, DC, then moved overseas to Vienna, Austria, then back to Washington, DC. From there, we moved across the country to the San Francisco Bay Area, then to St. Louis, MO, and then landed back in northern California, much to my delight. During that 20-year time span, I gave birth to and raised two wonderful children (a son and daughter) and started and ran several businesses.

WHAT I HAVE LEARNED IN BUSINESS:

1) Passion is infectious; it provides a strong motivation for entrepreneurs to achieve success;

2) There are ways to start and run a profitable company with little start-up investment;

3) Being focused on a specific goal means the difference between success and floundering;

4) If you can make friends, you can succeed in making sales;

5) Doing it all is a wonderful recipe for burnout;

6) People want to connect with companies and service providers that they trust;

7) Many people use their fears as an excuse; successful business owners do not; and

8) There will always be the newest and latest tools available for business growth, but nothing beats the basics.

BACK TO BUSINESS BASICS

Back to business basics inspired this book. In late 2008 and early 2009, I noticed that many small business owners were trying to add all sorts of new and wonderful business tools, but few were focusing on the basics of running a profitable business. That realization resulted in my presentation, *How to Grow Your Business in a Crappy Economy*, which I gave to groups of business owners in the San Francisco Bay Area and received a wonderful reception.

Comments from small- to medium-sized business owners reflected what I had seen: they had jumped on the newest "business tool" bandwagons at the expense of the tried-and-true business growth strategies, such as having a marketing plan with a clearly identified target market and then following it!

Many of the business owners that I encountered had gone to school or received training on the skills needed to serve clients, but had not learned business basics. They needed to learn how to market their goods and services to identifiable, viable potential clients and then to engage in meaningful interactions that resulted in sales.

If the days of "build it, and they will come" are gone, what is a business owner to do? We need to understand that the sales process is all about the connections you make with people—how well can you engage them? People do business with those they know, like, and trust. In other words, your prospects buy from people and businesses that they feel a connection to, and your job as a business owner is to develop that connection with enough viable prospects to make a profitable business.

The tools at your disposal are plentiful—that isn't the problem for most businesses. The problem is how to get the attention of and then keep the connection with your prospects, in other words, focus and engagement.

When I talked to business owners, I found that they had no real marketing plans. They were consumed with trying to accomplish 10, 15, and sometimes 20 different marketing strategies. They spent all of their time running their businesses, to the point that their businesses were running them. If something came up during their days that made them nervous or fearful, they avoided that activity and went onto something new—and with several dozen marketing strategies there was always something new to do. Most were talented at what they did, but few had put any time into thinking strategically about the growth of their businesses and what it would take to sustain a successful and profitable business. The constant worrisome and frightening news about the financial markets kept whipping up these business owners' fear, fury, and frustration.

BUILD THE BUSINESS YOU WANT FROM THE BUSINESS YOU HAVE

All business owners asked about time, life, and work balance. Many were overwhelmed and overloaded—and few received pleasure from running their businesses. So I developed a full-day seminar titled *Build the Business You Want From the Business You Have*, in which I taught marketing basics for small business owners.

This seminar starts with understanding why you run your business and what motivates you to keep going. Then it covers marketing, marketing plans, and what prevents you from marketing in meaningful ways to your prospects. Next, it focuses on developing a viable target market and then puts it all together in a marketing plan that you can follow. We end with some strategies to set boundaries so that you can have a life outside of running your business.

The seminars were a big success. Many business owners left and felt energized and enthusiastic to run their businesses in ways that they had forgotten. Here is some of the feedback I received from this program:

"I loved attending Heidi's workshop, 'Build the Business You Want from the Business You Have.' In a fun and empowering style, Heidi distills the nitty-gritty dos and don'ts of good marketing and shares great ways we can achieve a strong business-life balance. I left this workshop with a clearer vision of what I want my business to become and better focused on the steps I need to take to get there. Heidi is an excellent coach, a great motivator and, as an entrepreneur herself, a wonderful cheerleader. I would highly recommend her to any business owner who wants to drive their business (not the other way around!)."
- Sejal Parekh of Innovae Designs

"I ended up thoroughly enjoying this workshop, though initially I had reservations because business has always held a negative perception in my mind. I was blown away at the great command Heidi has of the material she presented. She was professional, straight to the point and delivered a lot of information in [a] short amount of time."
- Ana Maria Sanchez of Free the Light Within

"Wow! Heidi is clear, helpful, and inspiring. I loved the exercises, and the information was great. I highly recommend working with Heidi!"
- Kimi Avary, Dating and Relationship Coach of Your Dating and Relationship Success, http://YourDatingAndRelationshipSuccess.com

"Heidi's workshop covers a multitude of areas in marketing strategy and focus. The written materials are concise and the presentation interactive and engaging. I would highly recommend participation for any entrepreneur."
- Joanna Medin of PrePaid Legal Services

"Heidi's workshop was fun and informative with hands-on activities. [It was] great to take the time to focus on and plan marketing strategies for my business while away from the business. Love the intimate environment and sharing with other attendees."
- Judy Peebles of the Journaling Jenius

"There are so many marketing activities to choose from, Heidi's workshop helped me prioritize what I can do to benefit my business most." - Mimi Lam of State Farm Insurance

"This seminar changed my thoughts regarding marketing. Heidi provided valuable information, as well as inspiration to move my business forward." - Pat Raichlen of Intero Real Estate Services

"Heidi is full of concise constructive information that really gets you thinking about how you market your business. I have taken away some golden nuggets that will serve me well to improve my thinking about the power of selling and marketing my business."
- Jen Duchene of Lift Your Spirits Home Transformations, www.LYShome.com

My work, helping business owners understand what is needed to run a successful and profitable business, is very gratifying. I don't look to razzle-dazzle with new concepts, but rather I present tried-and-true business basics in such a way that leaves people feeling motivated and inspired. My goal for my program and this book is not to offer brand new ideas, but rather to package ideas in ways that make sense. I hope that you will see how you can run your businesses, make money, and have fun doing it.

I include the essence of what is in all of my seminars and programs in *Fortune is in the Follow-Up®* so that every business owner can have access to the business basics and easy-to-understand action steps that I teach—not just those in the San Francisco Bay Area. Good luck to you in growing your business. Making money should be fun and not a struggle—here's to your success!

Heidi BK Sloss

DEFINE YOUR TARGET MARKET

DEFINITION OF MARKETING

There are many definitions of marketing, but my favorite is to think of marketing as building a relationship with a prospect, or great referral source, until he or she feels comfortable enough to do business with you.

In other words, marketing is about building relationships. And most people need time and contact in order to build a meaningful relationship. Time invested in building a relationship with prospects will yield dividends by producing loyal customers and (hopefully) raving fans who spread the word about you and your company. Think of what success you would have if your current clients decided to tell everyone they know that doing business with you is terrific. How great would that be for you? Have you ever heard of the word "viral"? Yes, that's exactly what would happen.

MARKETING MODEL FOR SUCCESS

The marketing model I like clients to focus on is about building relationships. Strong relationships help you get new clients. It is also part of providing great customer service. Great customer service leads to more referrals, which means more business, which leads to higher prices, which means more money for you!

> Great customer service ➔
> leads to more referrals ➔
> means more business ➔
> leads to higher prices ➔
> leads to making more $!

The first step to move forward is to define WHO you want to do business with. In other words, who is your ideal client? This leads me to my first POWER strategy: **How to Define Your Target Market.**

DEFINITION OF TARGET MARKET

A great marketing plan starts with defining your target market. This is the population that you want to do business with. In other words, who are you marketing to? Since I defined marketing as building a relationship, then the beginning of your marketing plan helps you identify with whom you are building this relationship.

As we were working together, one of my real estate agent clients decided that she wanted to expand her business to include the referral real estate business. She wanted to work with both incoming and outgoing transferees who were being moved by their places of employment. Her marketing plan now included a focus on the human resource employees in the companies involved and not just the people being moved. She spent time thinking about who made the decisions to assist the transferees and then targeted those people in her marketing plan.

Another client, in the healthcare field, decided that the types of patients she wanted to work with would also work with chiropractors and physical therapists. So she started targeting both of these healthcare providers in her marketing plan.

In this day and age of specialties, most people want to hire a specialist. Think about when you have a medical problem. Do you want to go to a generalist or a specialist? Most will choose the specialist. That is one of the benefits of finding, defining, and then choosing a target market: that population knows you as the specialist.

Many business coaches also refer to this as defining, focusing, or developing your niche. This is a very powerful way to grow your business. If you develop the reputation for being the expert in a certain field, on a specific subject, or for a targeted population, you will differentiate yourself from your competition. This will allow you to present yourself from a position of power, strength, and confidence—all very attractive traits to your clients.

There are many reasons to develop a reputation as an expert for a well-defined position.

1) Experts make more money.

2) Experts command more respect.

3) Experts have more control of their businesses.

4) Experts are more in demand.

5) Experts are more powerful.

6) Marketing as an expert is more effective.

DEFINITION OF EFFECTIVE

You will notice that I use the word "effective" a lot. This is because many business owners work hard, but those who make

> **What is being effective? The definition is:**
>
> from: http://www.merriam-webster.com/dictionary/effective
> 1a : producing a decided, decisive, or desired effect <an effective policy>
>
> From: http://www.learnersdictionary.com/search/effective
> 1 [more ef*fec*tive; most ef*fec*tive] : producing a result that is wanted: having an intended effect
> It's a simple but effective technique. He gave an effective speech.
>
> From: http://www.brainyquote.com/words/ef/effective158450.html
> Having the power to produce an effect or effects; producing a decided or decisive effect; efficient;

money also work smart. What is the difference? Briefly, the main difference is those who can think, plan, and act strategically work smart; those who work many hours just work hard. Working smart is effective; working hard is draining. Growing a business does take work, and sometimes-hard work, but without smart work, most are just spinning their wheels in the sand. No task, activity, or project should be undertaken unless you can see that it will be effective for you to accomplish your goals and dreams. The key to accomplishment is all about being effective.

Anyone can start marketing or building a relationship with people, but is what you are doing effective? Is it producing the desired goal or effect? Are you having powerful results?

Picking a target market to focus on will make your marketing more effective and will save you both time and money—limited resources for most companies.

Think about this: If you only have to build relationships with a clearly defined target population, you will no longer have to spend your time and limited resources marketing to everyone. And the bottom line is that everyone is not a viable target market.

How can you possibly target everyone to develop a relationship with? Even if you chose to develop virtual relationships (using online marketing and sales techniques), you will still need to attract and develop relationships with your prospects.

If your marketing message is too general, you will lose your prospects to someone else who can speak to them by identifying their pain points and offering solutions that are in their language. In other words, your competitors will become their service provider or product supplier.

At a networking event I attended a few years ago, everyone introduced themselves and shared who was a good lead for them. A dermatologist took her turn, she stated that a good lead for her was everyone with skin. Of course, we all laughed, because it was funny. But afterward, I realized that it gave me no information about her practice or her specialty. Since my family had just moved back to the Bay Area, we were looking for a new dermatologist, but because she did not identify her target market, I was not sure which of my family members should see her. My husband needs help managing a long-standing skin disease. It is not serious, but does require ongoing medical treatment. At the time, both of my children were teenagers, each on different hormonal adventures, which means that each has a specific need for a dermatologist who specializes in teenagers and sports-related skin irritations. Finally, I have special needs, both as a post-menopausal woman and a skin-cancer survivor. Because she did not identify herself as a specialist in any of these areas, I didn't feel that she could provide the services we needed. Now the reality is that if she had identified just one specialty, one of us would have gone to see her. If just one had liked the experience of being her patient, we all would have wanted to see her, too. By being too broad in describing her target market, she missed out on treating a whole family with deep connections in the community.

Make note, having a focused target market does not mean that you serve or supply only the one market position you choose. It means that you focus your marketing only on one population, while continuing to provide services or goods to whoever contracts with you.

For example, I had a real estate client who wanted to gain traction in a competitive marketplace. She was going to focus on the condo market and become known as the "Condo Queen". She became the go-to person for anyone who was interested in buying or selling a condominium. She was able to articulate a big point of differentiation between herself and her competition. Did this mean that she was the only one who could help people buying or selling condos? Of course not, but she was able to limit her marketing dollars from chasing the ever-allusive market of "everyone" and instead just focus on marketing to those interested in buying or selling condominiums. Some of the wonderful outcomes of this focused strategy are: she attracted a lot more sellers who called her to help them sell their condos. This led to more buyer clients, some who were interested in buying condos and some interested in buying single-family homes—she never stopped working with people who were outside of her target market. She was able to grow her real estate practice exponentially by just focusing on marketing to one segment of the marketplace.

She was actually also able to turn down clients whom she identified as not viable. She was able to pick and chose who she wanted to work with, thereby increasing not only her bottom line, but also her level of work, happiness, and enjoyment.

Identifying an effective target market is one of the most mentally challenging tasks and requires discipline, time, and painstaking effort. Once you have a position, it becomes the driving force behind your entire marketing strategy.

> **"**It's important to continue to refine your target market, and at the same time, it's scary. Whether you've been in business for 1 year or 10 years or more, it feels like you are excluding a group. I suffered from this in my business, as well, when I first started. And I find that my clients are also challenged in this area ...
>
> I have found that when you attempt to speak to everybody, nobody listens. And when you get super crystal clear and focused on who you are best suited for, then actually, it does the opposite of what you think it's going to do. If you can define who your program, product, or service is the best fit for and if you can say that really succinctly and clearly, then the people who might not necessarily normally fit into the realm of who you would identify as your ideal client actually respond. And they respond to your clarity. And of course, just as importantly, the people who really do fit that model respond because you are speaking their language. You're talking directly and specifically to them, and that's important."
>
> - Sanyika Calloway Boyce of Sanyika Worldwide,
> http://tvpublicitysecrets.com

HOW TO SELECT A TARGET MARKET

Picking a target market involves finding a population of clients or customers who are viable for you. What does viable mean in this context? Think of viable as:

1) This population is accessible to you, and you are accessible to them.
2) This population is easily defined.
3) They have the money to spend on your services or products.

1) ACCESSIBILITY

Your target market needs to be accessible to you. If you are going to choose a certain population as your target market, you must make sure that you can get to them and they can get to you. You can choose to do business with anyone, but it will not be an effective choice if they are not accessible.

For instance, choosing to do business with seniors via the Internet might not be a viable choice for growing an online business. You want to make sure that you can reach your prospects and they can reach you. If you are selling services or products online, make sure that your target market has access to the Internet.

Keep in mind how accessible a population your target market is. For example, highly skilled and educated people, like attorneys and physicians, earn more money than other professionals. They become a highly desired target market for many business owners. But gaining access to attorneys or physicians is not easy. They usually have a high threshold that acts as a barrier and prevents people from approaching and marketing to them. If you want to pick a target market like this, I recommend that you have some connection in the fields of law or medicine to gain the access you need.

Take the time now to answer the following questions:

1) What groups of people or professions can you easily reach?

_____

_____

_____

_____

_____

2) What population do you know well and can gain access to?

_____

_____

_____

_____

_____

3) What population's buying habits do you know?

_____

_____

_____

_____

_____

4) What past experience do you have with different groups that you could use to gain access to?

_____

_____

_____

_____

_____

5) What connections or networks do you have that will help you reach a targeted population?

_____

_____

_____

_____

_____

2) EASILY DEFINED

The easier it is to define your target market, the easier it will be to reach them. If you cannot articulate who you are trying to build relationships with, how can you find them? How can others help you find them? The fact is most business owners grow their businesses through referrals, and people will refer new clients and customers to you IF they can easily talk about who you are and what you do. Your target market must be repeatable if you want to harness the power of referrals from people. Think about my previous example of the dermatologist—if she cannot identify her target market, how can anyone refer clients to her?

What makes a target market easily defined? Specificity and narrowness—the more specific and narrow you can limit your target market, the easier it will be to define and find it. This is a hallmark of viability.

I attended a workshop in which the presenter asked us to put together a short introduction for ourselves using only 140 characters—the same number used for putting a tweet on Twitter. Right now, put together an introduction for yourself using only 140 characters. Your introduction should tell your audience who you are, what you do, and who you do it with. Try it now:

_____

_____

_____

_____.

3) DO THEY HAVE DOLLARS?

Does your target market have money? This is critical for building a business. If you want to make money, you must pick a target market that has money and can and will spend it on you. Otherwise, you will just have a great idea with no market.

One of my former clients wanted to set up a service business as a life coach for stay-at-home mothers. She had great past experience as a stay-at-home mother, connections from her previous background,

> **❝❞I** believe in having client avatars to help me visualize who my ideal clients are. Having my client avatar has made a huge difference for me because I can say no. There are a lot of groups out there that want a speaker, but if they're not in my client demographic, I know that when I present my offer, they won't be able to afford it. There's no reason for me to play in those circles if they're not going to be able to afford my services. So I can say no to some speaking opportunities. Speaking for free is part of my marketing plan. I want to speak for free in front of people who are in my demographic. If they aren't, I found that it's been a waste of time. I'm interested in meeting new people, but I need to meet new people who are like my client avatar. I have to look at my time as money so I can make sure that my effort is focused and I am reaching my ideal demographic."
>
> - Alicia Dunams of Bestseller in a Weekend,
> www.bestsellerinaweekend.com

and was able to easily define this target market and their needs, but she forgot to research how much money they tend to spend on these services. After doing that research, she quickly learned that the stay-at-home mother market was not willing to spend money on her proposed service. So she instead offered her services to a population that was willing to spend money on coaching services. Instead of working with stay-at-home mothers, she chose to work with women who were trying to balance employment and motherhood—a population with an identifiable need—lifestyle balance—and money AND a willingness to spend it.

Exercise: Define your target market: Who do you work with? Why them?

List your clients for the last 6 to 12 months in the first column below. On a scale of 1 to 10, rank how 'ideal' those clients are for your business. A 10 means they were great clients for your business, and 1 means that they were not. Think about:

1) Were they easy to work with?
2) Did they love what you had to offer to them?
3) Did you have to put together new products or services for them, or did they contract with your company's offerings as is?
4) How did the transactions go? Easy or stressful? Why?

CLIENTS	1	2	3	4	5	6	7	8	9	10

Now state your reasons for the ranking you gave each client.

_____

_____

_____

_____

_____

Next, do you see a pattern? What do your highest-ranking clients have in common? Is it:

Age	Life-Style Stage	Social Class
Income	Age of Children	Personality Trait
Occupation	Social Club	Sports Activities
Education	Residence	Religion
Cultural Activities	Location	Hobbies
Career Stage	Price Range	Social Activities

Once you see a pattern, you can begin to identify your target market. What do you know about them? The more you are able to describe your target market, the better. You will use this information to help build relationships with your target market. If you had difficulty writing your introduction using only 140 characters before, go back, and try it again now that you have defined and narrowed your target market description.

_____

_____

_____

_____.

A SINGLE FOCUSED POSITION

The most effective marketing plans are built around a single focused position that you have staked out in marketing messages to your prospects. If done properly, it will clearly differentiate you from your competition, which will make marketing much more effective.

The concept of positioning is such a deceivingly simple concept that most entrepreneurs fail to comprehend how powerful it is. Understand that marketing material is not slapping your name, photo, and logo onto some standard marketing format. The secret is to make your information stand for one distinctive thing that will give you a competitive advantage of being remembered. The essence of marketing is establishing a mental HOOK in your clients' minds.

From Ried and Trout's book, *Positioning*:

a. You must position yourself in your prospect's mind.

b. Your position must differentiate you from your competition.

c. You must be willing to sacrifice part of the marketplace. You cannot be all things to all people.

"I have run my own business for the past 17 years. But back when we began, we did not have either a marketing plan or an identified target market. We started the initial business with the spaghetti method: without a plan, throwing everything against the wall to see what stuck. We sought out a variety of clients to whom to pitch our services. Our plan was to see 5 new clients per day—amazingly, it worked and we started acquiring clients. This, of course, was before the dependence on computers—everything we did was on a personal level—meetings, phone calls, etc.

Once we began to have customers, we were able to identify, more specifically, our target markets. We began to identify patterns—the kinds of customers who needed our guidance, expertise, and products. At that point, we were able to fine-tune our offerings and customer outreach.

About six years ago, I started to approach my business with a much more professional attitude—times in business had clearly changed. I used the services of SCORE, part of the SBA, to set up a business and marketing plan. This was the best investment of time that I could have made.

Putting my plan together helped me to organize my time, intent, and target market. I am now able to define who I want for new clients. This has allowed me to save time and energy—both limited resources! I now avoid calls to prospects who are not appropriate for our accessory line."

- Karen Korman/President, Marketing Action Xecutives, Inc.
www.seeandbesafe.com

8 QUESTIONS TO ASK YOURSELF WHEN SELECTING
A TARGET MARKET

Finding the right target market will make the difference between the success and failure of your marketing plan. Don't skimp on the time it takes to define a viable target market. Ask yourself:

1) What population do I have access to?
2) Are they easily defined?
3) Can I refer to this group easily when describing them to referral sources?
4) Do they have the money to spend on my goods or services?
5) Are they part of my background experiences?
6) Are they part of my connections or network?
7) Do I like this population well enough to want to spend my time learning about them, connecting with them, and helping them?
8) Do I know their buying habits, tastes, and preferences?

ACTION ITEMS:
Conduct Target Market Research

Part of being an effective business owner is conducting target market research. What does your target market need? What do they want? What is missing for them? Learn about their buying habits, and their spending patterns. Then you can start figuring out a way to communicate effectively with them, which will help you to build a relationship with them so that they feel comfortable enough to do business with you.

1) **Pick some prospects to contact** and ask them if they would take your 10 to 20 minute research survey. Make sure that they know that this is not a sales pitch—promise them that. Tell them that this is strictly research. Period.

2) **Telephone or in-person research only.** Do not email your questions, and do not set this up as an online survey. This must be done in real time, either in person or on the phone. You need to make the connection with your potential target market and be able to listen and learn from them directly. You can hire a company to do research AFTER you have done some of the work yourself. If you are resisting this exercise, ask yourself 1) if running a business is right for you, and 2) if this population is one that you like well enough to work with.

3) **Develop the questions you will use to research your target market.** Here are 11 questions to consider using. Some of the questions might seem repetitive; use them only if the previous question did not get much of a response.

11 QUESTIONS TO ASK YOUR TARGET MARKET

1) Who is your current service provider, or where do you purchase the following goods?
2) What do/did you like about doing business with them?
3) What don't/didn't you like about doing business with them?
4) What would your ideal provider/supplier do for you?
5) What are you looking for in a provider/supplier?
6) What are your goals or desires or reasons or motivation for hiring a [fill in your profession]?
7) What do you want to achieve or accomplish when you hire a [fill in your profession]?
8) What do you worry about when hiring a [fill in your profession]?
9) What excites you about [fill in from the answer to #7]?
10) What is missing for you from your current service provider/supplier?
11) How can a [fill in your profession] best meet your needs?

Fortune is in the Follow-Up®:
Mass appeal equals no appeal. Most entrepreneurs are terrified by the thought of sacrificing part of their marketplace. They mistakenly believe that if they do, they will limit their opportunities. The reality is that by narrowing your appeal, you dramatically increase the strength of your appeal, which makes it much easier to attract clients.

BONUS CHAPTER: HOW TO CREATE A MARKETING PLAN

No matter what you are trying to accomplish, you need to plan for it to happen. I am a huge fan of marketing plans. I know that many business coaches and marketing gurus teach and talk about business plans. While business plans have their place, I think that a marketing plan is more useful for most small business owners. A business plan is important for companies that are trying to secure funding; however, not all businesses need outside funding. And even after a company has sought outside funding, they still need a marketing plan to tell them who they are trying to do business with and how they will do it. I like marketing plans because they are action-oriented with a purpose!

DEFINITION OF A MARKETING PLAN

A marketing plan is like a roadmap. It tells you where you want to go and how to get there. Without a map, you might still get to your destination, but not very effectively. Think about a road trip

> 66Marketing creates visibility. And visibility is the key to making more money. If you're not visible, then how do people know to buy from you? So, I think the biggest thing in my marketing plan is it keeps me visible. It keeps my name on the lips of people in terms of that. I had a call this morning from somebody who had somebody else say to her, 'You need to meet Ann Evanston.' And that, to me is what a good marketing plan does. Marketing creates opportunity, which to me is something like that example and what I'm doing with you. It's that way of keeping that visibility of who you are and what you do in the hearts and minds of people."
>
> - Ann Evanston of Warrior-Preneur, www.warrior-preneur.com

that will require three or four days of driving. Without a map or a GPS, it might take you months and months of driving. It will involve stopping and starting and asking for directions (if you are a woman). Do you have months to spend on a task that would only take you a few days if you had a plan? The obvious answer is no, most of us do not have extra time to waste.

With a marketing plan in place, you will know: 1) who you are marketing to, 2) what activities you need to do to reach those people, and 3) where you will connect with them.

WHY YOU NEED A MARKETING PLAN

1) A marketing plan gives you direction, and this helps you achieve your goals more effectively. Without a marketing plan, you will find it easier to get distracted and harder to keep focused on your goals.

2) A clear set of marketing activities helps prevent burnout. Getting overwhelmed is very easy when running a business. Your plan will keep you on track and moving forward.

3) With the advent of MeetUp.com and other online networking resources, there are many more in-person marketing opportunities than ever before. Knowing which opportunities are right for you AND making sure that you spend your limited resources reaching your intended target market is best accomplished by having a marketing plan in place.

4) Many business owners have an idea of what they would like to see happen in the future. But few actually take the time to put their dreams on paper. What would you like to see your business accomplish in the next 12 months? What about the next 3 to 5 years? Having a concrete marketing plan with specific action items will make all the difference. Working the activities in your marketing plan means less tangential time-sucks and more

❝I use my marketing plan to get a big picture view. I call it getting in the helicopter and getting a big picture view. One of the biggest challenges I find for myself and my clients is that so often we're so busy working in the business that working on the business becomes way, way, way backburner. We look up and realize we haven't achieved certain things or we haven't really moved the ball forward.

So a marketing plan really helps me to get clear and focused on what it is that I need to be doing, especially as it relates to working on my business, so that I'm moving it forward and not so stuck on anything like checking emails, returning client calls, or doing any of those administrative things that can crowd out and drown out the bigger picture.❞

- Sanyika Calloway Boyce of Sanyika Worldwide, http://tvpublicitysecrets.com

meaningful and productive activities that will help you reach your goals and grow your business.

PUTTING IT TOGETHER

How do you put together your marketing plan, now that you have your target market identified? Start with remembering the definition of marketing:

Marketing is building a relationship with a prospect or great referral source until they feel comfortable enough to do business with you.

After you define WHO you want to target, the next task is to figure out HOW you are going to reach them. This requires thinking about WHERE they are.

1) Where do they hang out?

2) Where do they get information?

3) Where do they shop?

4) Where do they learn?

5) What associations do they belong to?

See the Action Items from **Power Strategy One: How to Define Your Target Market** for ideas on how to conduct Target Market Research.

"When our business was young, I confused 'marketing' with 'advertising'. I knew most of our business came from referrals. Since we did beautiful, quality work and had many happy clients and raving fans, I believed that by occasionally advertising in a magazine or in a directory, we were doing all we needed to keep business in the pipeline. Times were good, and the business was growing—I thought, we must be doing something right!

Then the dot-com bomb hit Silicon Valley like the atom bomb and set just about every business in the area reeling. We all had to look at, and embrace, change, if we were going to survive. Working with a marketing coach, we developed a 'Strategic Marketing Plan'. In retrospect, that was the most important and best thing we could have chosen to do then, as well as for the long-term sustainability of our company, which is now celebrating over 20 years of business.

We were not trained in marketing and had not been 'business majors' in college. We were artists and artisans designing and building beautiful home environments and nurturing and taking care of our clients so that they realized their dreams with as little stress as possible! We knew all about developing and carrying out architectural plans, but definitely not marketing plans!

To put together our marketing plan, we researched our competition, looking at what was working and not working, in terms of collateral, websites, and positioning in the community. We identified our target markets and really fleshed them out to see exactly who they were and what made them tick on every level. We looked at all the different 'tactics' we were currently using to reach our target market, and we also looked at some of the opportunities we were missing that seemed to be successful for our competition. We looked at the hard costs of different marketing tactics to see if the R.O.I. (return on investment) was really worth the investment of both time and money. Working with our marketing coach was like working with an 'image consultant' for the entire business, and it involved introductions to other professionals like graphic designers and web developers to bring our image up to the standard of the quality of work and service that we were providing to our clients.

And then the really fun part kicked in. We held companywide staff meetings to brainstorm ideas for the direction our company would take.

This included a new company name, logo, mission statement, tagline, collateral, and website—a whole new and consistent image. With this brainstorming process, so many creative ideas came forth, along with several new tactics to get the word out about our company. The added bonus of this process was the teambuilding that took place and the solidifying of the company culture of collaboration, communication, and respect that is so much a part of Spectrum Fine Homes, Inc. today.

Wearing my new hat as marketing director, I revisited our Strategic Marketing Plan once a month to monitor the results of our efforts, and keep current with what was happening in the market in terms of our competitors and our target markets. I would make adjustments if needed, and this also gave me ammunition to be able to say 'yes' or 'no' to solicitations for paid advertising or participation in time-consuming community events. If it didn't fit our mission, our plan, our position, or our budget, I would immediately know and not feel guilty for saying no. If it looked like there was a great fit, then I could make a quick decision and act in a timely way to reap the benefits of the offer.

As I became more involved with reviewing, revising, and implementing our Strategic Marketing Plan, I also became more excited about being the marketing director. As the social-media world started to develop, I saw this as a very important piece of the overall strategy we had developed. Since it was a new and different way of operating, I saw the opportunity to get on board to position our company, and my own passions for my industry, on a much broader scale. Being active on the Internet with social media was also important because our well-defined target market was composed largely of a demographic very involved in the social-media world. Incorporating some new concepts and tactics was easy, because we already had the Strategic Marketing Plan in place, and introducing new ideas was already part of our system of operation.

The results of this process of coaching, collaborating, learning, and changing with the times, has led to much more than growing and positioning our business. It has also resulted in developing a company culture and true success in our business, where our values and mission are what we are known for by our evolving target market and beyond. I believe having a strategy that is ever-evolving and improving will always contribute to the viability of any company!"

– Susan M. Davis of GreenPoint Coach

MARKETING PLAN STRATEGIES

Don't limit yourself to thinking that marketing is the same as advertising. Advertising is one of hundreds of ways to market to your target market, and frequently, is it not the most effective way to do so. There are many other great options available today.

I love the Guerrilla Marketing series by Jay Conrad Levinson and Al Lautenslager. Their *Guerrilla Marketing in 30 Days* book is a fabulous resource of ideas to get your marketing "mojo" going. Their website has a treasure chest of ideas on how to connect with your prospects. One of their many resource lists is called the 200 Marketing Weapons (http://www.gmarketing.com/articles/5-100-marketing-weapons). Most of these items are free or at a very low cost, which is always helpful when budgeting for your marketing activities. To read a transcript of my interview with Jay Conrad Levinson, noted speaker and author of *Guerrilla Marketing*, go to: http://www.fortuneisinthefollowup.net/readers-special-gift.

One word of caution when picking strategies for your marketing plan: It is important to pick enough strategies that will help you connect and build relationships with your target marketing, but not so many that you get overwhelmed. I advise that you pick just a few strategies and commit to them for a period of time of at least 9 months, ideally 12 months. Go narrow and deep, rather than shallow and wide. This approach will allow you to do them well, make adjustments as you go along, and not be distracted or overwhelmed with more than you can handle.

Chasing the latest-and-greatest marketing strategies is a never-ending, losing game. If you are constantly trying one tool and then abandoning it after a few weeks or even months, you will never gain the traction you need to build your marketing momentum. Too often, business owners come to me complaining that a particular marketing strategy won't work for their business, when they really mean it didn't work for them the first or second time they tried it, so they gave up and tried something new.

How do you pick which strategies to focus on? You will need to think big picture and focus on strategies that will give you the most bang for your buck. Most business owners do not spend nearly enough time on business planning, and this is one of the most important activities you will need to do to grow your business effectively (my favorite word!). Many owners complain that they do not have time or money to remove themselves from their daily work on the business. But strategizing on how to reach the right population by using the right marketing tools will save you time and money, both in the short and long term.

There are no shortcuts when focusing on your marketing plan. It will take time to put one together—time best spent away from your business, thinking and strategizing. If you feel like you do not have the time to spend on this, calendar it into your schedule and do not reschedule it.

This pattern of constantly trying different marketing strategies will cost you time, money, and energy—something that few business owners

> **❝**I refer to my marketing plan at least once a month. I check it to see: 1) what my focus is this month, 2) what I need to do to make sure my intended outcomes happen, 3) what I am supposed to be working on, and 4) what I haven't worked on that I said I was going to last month. Instead of figuring out what should I be doing, the answer is usually already there. I use my plan to remind myself, 'Oh! Go back to your plan.'
>
> It's so easy to get off course or start down a road and not necessarily remember why you started down that road in the first place. So get on the path and then check in to see, okay, why am I on this path? Does this path still make sense, and what should I be doing differently or that I haven't done?
>
> – Sanyika Calloway Boyce of Sanyika Worldwide,
> http://tvpublicitysecrets.com

can waste. Instead of running after the latest marketing strategies, take some time away from your business, to develop a thoughtful marketing plan that has a few chosen strategies that will get you maximum exposure to your target market for the least amount of money.

I have to admit I am biased. I think that a business coach who specializes in marketing plans is a fabulous resource for business owners to strategize how best to reach their target markets. Helping you to be effective, efficient, and productive for your marketing activities, a business coach will help save you time, money, and energy.

HOW TO CHOOSE A BUSINESS COACH

It is not in the scope of this book to help you choose the right business coach for you, but there are a few basic considerations to keep in mind when selecting your support team.

1) Find someone with the right background or experience. Anyone can learn about marketing from all sorts of sources these days, so you want to find someone who has "been there and done that."

2) Find someone who you can relate to.

3) You want someone who can articulate their ideas to you in motivating ways that you can understand. Most of what you will need is not about reinventing the wheel; but it is important that you pick someone who puts the ideas and concepts into words that you can hear, take in, and then put into an action plan that you will follow.

HOW MUCH TO INVEST IN YOUR MARKETING

Since we know that marketing takes time and sometimes money, the next considerations are: 1) how much time you should spend on marketing, and 2) how much money you should spend on marketing.

66 I absolutely have a marketing plan. I'm a big believer that most small business owners get in trouble on this. I joke about what I call the marketing rollercoaster. This is that many small business owners only market when they need customers, and when it's smooth sailing on the ride, they stop marketing. That's really when they should be marketing so that the flow of business is steady and they're not on that crazy rollercoaster ride. I do a one-year marketing plan once a year. My team is highly involved in that."

— Ann Evanston of Warrior-Preneur, www.warrior-preneur.com

HOW MUCH TIME YOU SHOULD SPEND ON MARKETING

First, let's talk about how much time you should spend on marketing activities. For the purposes of this book, I refer to marketing as ALL those activities that are designed to help you build relationships with your prospects. So that means *any time* you spend talking about your business or work, putting together your marketing plans, or strategizing how you will connect with prospects counts as marketing time. That said, I recommend you spend 75 percent of your time on marketing your business. Spend the remaining 25 percent on your top clients.

If that recommendation nearly made you fall over in your chair, you are in good company. Many business owners have a very strong reaction to it. But as Malcolm Gladwell wrote in his bestselling book, *Outliers,* "Ten thousand hours is the magic number of greatness." [Page 41, Little, Brown and Company, November 2008 edition] That means you must invest time in what you are doing if you want to see it pay back in results. *Outliers* goes on to quote neurologist Daniel Levitin [page 40], "The emerging picture ... is that ten thousand hours of practice is required to achieve the level of mastery associated with being a world-class expert—in anything."

Now, most business owners did not choose to become marketing experts when they started their businesses. But the fact of the matter is that you must become one now if you want to grow your business. You don't have to invest 10,000 hours in marketing; however, you do have to invest a significant chunk of time if you want to make money—for most business owners that means probably more than you are currently spending.

Where does that leave you? Well, as we talked about earlier, you want to pick a target market and then become their

> **❝** I think some of the best advice that I've gotten is that you're the marketer of your business, not the doer of your business. That you should work on your business and not in your business. The marketing of a product or service is more important than the service and product itself. It is critical to know that marketing is the essential to growing your business."
>
> —Alicia Dunams of Bestseller in a Weekend,
> www.bestsellerinaweekend.com

expert—remember experts make more money! So if you want to be your target market's expert, you will need to put in the time, and that means marketing a lot to them. Devoting 75 percent of your time to marketing means that you will not only become your target market's expert, but also you will see the financial rewards.

The other way I like to approach this is to remind clients that once they started their companies, marketing became their business. In fact, marketing becomes your livelihood, and your success is tied to your marketing efforts. Period.

The most frequent response to my 75 percent recommendation, after shock, is to question how that is possible, given the limited number of hours in a day and the number of hours it takes to run a business and serve your customers. That is a very reasonable question, and the response is that it is not possible. You cannot do it all, and you cannot be it all. There are only so many hours and only so much effort you can devote to grow your business. You need time for your health and personal life, too. "All work and no play makes Jack a dull boy" is not far from the truth.

What is a person to do? Well, the next chapter in this book is called **3 Secrets of Successful Delegation**. I suppose you can figure out my number one solution to this dilemma!

HOW MUCH MONEY YOU SHOULD SPEND ON MARKETING

The next question clients ask a lot is, "How much money should be spent on marketing a business?" There is no one formula I recommend; however, if you look at marketing as an expense, rather than an investment, it will show up on your financial reports as a large entry. Is marketing an expense or an investment for you? The difference is significant. If you approach marketing as an investment, then you will see the rewards of this investment grow when you think strategically about marketing. If you see marketing as one big fat expense line item, you will have a hard time growing your business profitably. Too many business owners do not plan for their marketing investment and then find growth almost impossible.

When I started my real estate business in the Midwest, we were new to the area and knew very few people in town. Building a thriving real estate practice is all about who you know. I was at a distinct disadvantage for the business. So what did I do? I invested my marketing money to build a name and reputation for myself using the local weekly town newspapers. I advertised on a regular basis, being consistent with both the frequency and marketing message. And in a few months, it started to work. Did anyone ever hire me just from my newspaper ads? No, of course not. So how did I know it was working? By how people reacted to me when we first met. More often than not, when I was first introduced, people told me that they were sure they knew me. Since we were new in town, this was impossible; I knew it came from regularly seeing my advertisements in the paper.

NUTS AND BOLTS OF MARKETING DOLLARS

Many marketing experts have a percentage of gross revenue that they like to suggest to business owners to allocate for marketing budgets. Part of determining your marketing budget involves how many years you are in business and how fast and how large you are prepared and ready to grow.

Newer businesses will need to spend more on marketing than established businesses. And those ready for growth can continue to spend more as they can handle more clients. While every company and marketing budget are different, some marketing budget information is common:

1. Most small businesses spend anywhere from 2 percent to 10 percent of sales on marketing.

2. Medium-sized businesses tend to spend 10 percent or more.

3. Large companies, retailers, pharmaceutical companies and the like often spend upward of 20 percent of their revenue on marketing and advertising.

Important questions to answer:

1. How many more clients are you able to handle at this minute?

2. What if you suddenly doubled the number of clients you had?

3. Do you have the time and infrastructure to handle this?

Note: grow too fast and you will not succeed. It takes infrastructure development and systems to be able to handle an influx of new clients. Many business owners think they would be able to deal with this "problem" were it to occur, but the reality is it could prevent you from handling both your current and new clients in a sustainable way. Dropping the ball on customer service is a great way to business failure, something that none of us want to see or experience. We explore how to grow your business into profitability via great customer service in Power Strategy 4: **7 Stellar Customer Service Strategies.**

I recommend that business owners approach their marketing budget as a business investment, much like buying a large piece of equipment or expanding/renovating their locations. Unfortunately, too many business owners under spend on marketing, thinking that not spending is the same as saving. This is not correct. The expression, "You've got to spend money to make money," is true. The critical element is to make sure that your marketing dollars are spent on **effective strategies,** aimed at your target market and/or great referral sources that know, work, and touch your target market.

If you think that your marketing budget will be taken from your net profit after all other expenses are taken care of, you will not grow. The bottom line is that your marketing efforts have a direct bearing on your revenue.

According to marketing guru, Jay Levinson, in his *Guerrilla Marketing in 30 Days,* 2nd Edition, "The Small Business Administration (SBA) says that 'two of the main reasons small businesses fail is undercapitalization and the absence of effective marketing programs.' Many marketing programs aren't effective because they, too, are undercapitalized." [Page 263] Note the use of the word effective!

While I cannot tell you how much you should spend on marketing, I can tell you that how good you are at what you do has little to do with how many clients you have or how much money you make. What determines your success is how well you market, that is, how well you are able to build relationships and engage with your target market.

Have you ever seen successful companies that offer only medium-quality products or services? And have you also watched companies that offer great-quality goods or services go out of business? What was the difference? Their marketing! If you want your business to succeed, it will take marketing actions from you, which will cost both time and financial resources; but the rewards will be worth it. Owning a growing and successful business that allows you to live your dream life is wonderful!

66 One of the blessings and the curses of how fast the world is moving is it is moving fast, and there's always new, exciting things to do, and it can be done as it relates to marketing. The challenge is that not all of [the strategies and tactics] should be done.

I tend to work with and attract the type of business owners who I call 'bright-shiny-object' people. And that's because I'm one, too. These are people who hear of a new activity or project or tool and think, 'Oh, this is really cool.' Or, 'That's really pretty.' Or, 'Let's look at that.' And whenever the new thing flashes and sparkles, that's where our attention goes. I've used my marketing plan to remind me (and my clients) that just because everybody says I'm supposed to be on Twitter, LinkedIn, Facebook, or whatever the newest thing is, it doesn't particularly mean that that's where I should be focusing my energy.

And while it might be a cool new thing and everybody seems to be coming out with advertisements saying how they made a million dollars in their sleep on LinkedIn, is that really where your clients are going to be found? Is a Twitter strategy going to be an effective strategy for you? And so, going back to the desired outcome is important. I have to remind myself and my clients to think about what it is we really want.

– Sanyika Calloway Boyce of Sanyika Worldwide,
http://tvpublicitysecrets.com

HOW TO CREATE A MARKETING PLAN

Once you have identified a viable target market, you need to think about how you will reach them. Where do they hang out? What associations do they belong to? Where do they network? Where do they shop? Where do they learn? Who else does business with them? For some of you, making direct connections will not work as easily as making contact with great referral sources with others who work with your target market—like mortgage brokers and real estate agents, or real estate agents and divorce attorneys, or financial planners and attorneys, or chiropractors and acupuncturists, or fitness trainers and physical therapists, or party planners and caterers.

Now that you have a clearly defined target market and some ideas on how to reach them from Power Strategy One, you can use the worksheet on the following pages to put together a marketing plan. I have put in sample strategies, but use the strategies that get you to your target market best.

SAMPLE MARKETING PLAN

My Target Market (TM) is: Make sure you have a concise description of your target market—think 140 characters!

STRATEGY 1: WEBSITE
- Build a website—keeping in mind your TM.
- *NOTE: best to hire a website designer*
- Add keywords. *NOTE: Best to hire a website designer*
- Add a blog to your website. Get traction by making comments on other industry leaders' blogs.
- Use language that appeals to your TM
- Make offers that appeal to your TM

- Research places to promote your website—where does your TM look? *NOTE: best to hire a social-media expert.*

STRATEGY 2: NETWORKING
- Pick networking groups that put you in direct contact w/your TM
- Pick networking groups that put you in contact w/great referral sources (who work with and /or touch your TM)
- Calendar all the events for the year for your networking groups
- Develop 15, 30 and 60 seconds intros that explain what you do and for whom
- Calendar time for your one-on-ones

STRATEGY 3: FOLLOW-UP
- Calendar time for follow-up daily or weekly
- Commit to a set number of calls per week. Want to super charge? Make at least 5 a week!
- Blog regularly in forums that your target market reads.
- Commit to a set number of meetings per week—share info about your business and get info about theirs
- Go into any meeting with the "How-can-I-help?" attitude
- Report to your business coach (or accountability partner)

STRATEGY 4: PUBLIC RELATIONS
- Learn what info interests/excites your TM
- Tell a compelling story about why your prospects should do business w/you. What makes you the more interesting?
- *NOTE: Best to hire a media and/or PR specialist*
- Write a media pitch and/or press release
- *NOTE: Best to hire a media and/or PR specialist*

- Research media outlets and send your pitch/press release to your researched media list.
- *NOTE: Best to hire a virtual assistant to do this research*
- Follow-up your pitch/release with phone calls.
- *NOTE: Best to hire a virtual assistant to do this*

STRATEGY 5: PUBLIC SPEAKING

- Pick organizations, associations, groups, etc. that puts you in direct contact w/your TM
- Pick organizations, associations, groups, etc. that puts you in contact with great referral sources (who work with and/or touch your TM)
- Start a blogging campaign to grow your contact list and establish yourself as an industry expert
- Develop 3 speaking presentations that will appeal to your TM, show you as an expert
- Put together a speaker one-sheet—this lists short blurb about your topics and about you. Group may use this info to promote your presentation

STRATEGY 6: JOINT VENTURES

- Research who works with your TM
- *NOTE: Best to hire a virtual assistant to do this research*
- Meet with potential Joint Venture Partners to discuss possible joint projects and/or offers

STRATEGY 7: WHAT ELSE?

_____

_____

_____

❝I tend to focus on four activities. And if you really look at them strategically, other than networking, which I really only do maybe once a month, they all overlap and that's the key. [Activities] that I can overlap and I can repurpose and reuse them in multiple ways. So for me, that's why those four work well. The hardest part with marketing is if you are your brand in your business and people are deciding whether or not they're going to hire you, you need to be a part of your marketing. Your voice has to be there. And if you outsource that, you're going to find that it's not your voice.❞

— Ann Evanston of Warrior-Preneur, www.warrior-preneur.com

MARKETING STRATEGY IDEAS:

a. Effective networking

b. Make calls: cold and warm

c. Public speaking

d. Workshops/seminars

e. eNewsletters

f. Articles

g. Blog

h. Videos

i. Publishing

j. Public relations

k. Direct mail

l. Internet presence

m. Advertising

n. Multi-media

o. Strategic alliances

p. Joint Ventures

q. What else?

Very important: Pick only 4 to 8 strategies to work on at a time.

Fortune is in the Follow-Up®:
A marketing plan is like your business GPS. Make sure you program it correctly with the right target market and marketing strategies so that it will get you to your destination.

3 SECRETS OF SUCCESSFUL DELEGATION

"Asking for help is not cheating.
It's how anything important gets done."
C.J. Hayden, *Get Clients Now*, 2nd Edition.

Someone once said that one cannot have it all, and while that may or may not be so, it is true that we cannot do it all—certainly not all at once!

REALISTIC VERSUS UNREALISTIC TIME CONSTRAINTS

All too frequently, business owners spend many waking hours trying to figure out how to get everything done. They act as if they do not believe that there is a limit to what and how much they can do in one 24-hour period. They mistakenly believe that if they were just more efficient or more productive, they would be able to accomplish more. While I have noticed that many business owners waste a significant amount of time and energy (and to some extent money), the bigger issue is the unrealistic expectations that they place on themselves.

Too many business owners believe that it is possible to cram more tasks, more projects, and more items on their to-do lists, and that once that happens, all will fall into place. This belief is not only unrealistic, but also impossible. There really are only 24 hours in a day, and we all need some of those hours for sleep. Biologically, we need some downtime, some time when we are not working.

> 66 The things that I don't mind necessarily doing in the business, and when you start out there's these little tedious things that you do, those were a little harder to let go of. I realized that I needed to let go of them so that I could, (A) market better, and (B) be more visible in my business. If I am the brand that people hire, then they need to know me. And if I'm caught up in all this little tedious stuff, it just doesn't work."
>
> – Ann Evanston of Warrior-Preneur, www.warrior-preneur.com

Rest and recovery downtime is part of what everyone needs, but few business owners take. I know many Type A people, who are taking nice, big juicy bites out of life. I support their enthusiasm and passion for what they are doing. However, no one can sustain high-quality work with little or no downtime. In fact, it is downtime that allows for our creative juices to flow. And if you want to run a thriving and profitable business, you need all your creativity to be working. Business owners need to be able to creatively handle all sorts of challenges and opportunities.

> **❝** I think delegating is probably one of the most challenging and frustrating things that entrepreneurs do, especially if you are your brand. If you are the kind of 'boot-strapped-it, chief cook, and the bottle washer' entrepreneur, it's very difficult to relinquish control. I find that the reason that we have a hard time delegating is because of a lack of systems and a lack of documenting the things that we do almost instinctively, almost naturally as solopreneurs as we're evolving to the next level of who we are as owners of businesses."
>
> — Sanyika Calloway Boyce of Sanyika Worldwide, http://tvpublicitysecrets.com

As a business owner, here are just a few of the many situations when you need creativity:

- Taking great care of your clients/customers (see Chapter Four: **7 Stellar Customer Service Strategies** for more on this one)
- Overcoming prospects' objections
- Figuring out how to find, reach, connect, and engage with your prospects in a meaningful way
- Knowing how best to pitch prospects so that you show how your company knows about and solves their problems
- Creating marketing strategies that appeal to your target market
- Identifying new and emerging target markets
- Finding and developing power partners for joint ventures
- Identifying new products and/or services for your target market
- Finding better quality, less expensive ways to meet the needs of your clients
- Inspiring and directing employees.

Too often, though, business owners use too much creative brainpower working on administrative tasks, and this prevents them from thinking, strategizing, and approaching their businesses from the big picture. IS this you?

I see many business owners who do not understand how to find balance in their lives. I referenced the 10,000 hours to be an expert quote from Malcolm Gladwell's *Outliers* book in the previous chapter, but there is nothing in any of the literature about doing the 10,000 hours all at once!

> **66** Anybody who tells me they don't have time, just hasn't decided they value it enough. Because I have people who ask me, 'How do you have time for everything you do?' Well, I value it, so I make the time. I make time for my business. I make time for my clients. I make time for my relationship. I make time for my home. I make time for my wine. I make time to go to the gym. I value it so I find the time, and it's there."
>
> – Ann Evanston of Warrior-Preneur, www.warrior-preneur.com

There are enough hours in the day to do what you need to get done, and there are enough hours in the day to be productive IF you focus on the right things. I love to tell people that everyone really does have enough time to do everything that is important to them, the hard part is figuring out what is important!

PRIORITIES ON YOUR TIME

This means making priorities. This means taking the time to think about what your business needs to grow and what it needs from YOU specifically.

Finding think time is critical for business owners. Most just launch into the most immediate problem or task before them, but in doing so, they are not strategically positioning themselves to make the most of the time that they have. In his bestselling book, *7 Habits of Highly Effective People*, Stephen Covey shares his time-management matrix chart, outlining the difference between urgent and important tasks in your day.

	Urgent	Not Urgent
Important	**I** - Crisis - Pressing issues - Deadlines - Meetings	**II** - Preparation - Planning - Prevention - Relationship building - Personal development
Not Important	**III** - Interruptions - Some mail - Many popular activities	**IV** - Trivia - Some phone calls - Excessive TV/Games - Time wasters

Too often, business owners get sidetracked by urgent but not important tasks (box III), leaving not enough time in the important but not urgent (box II), which leads to always feeling pressed into adding items that are urgent and important (box I). Sometimes to give themselves a break, they then start working on not important and not urgent (box IV) tasks as a way to feel like they are getting something done.

Do you find yourself feeling like a ball in a pinball machine, constantly getting batted around by someone else at the controls? As a way to cross something off your to-do list at the end of the day, do you focus on those small, seemingly easy and short tasks just so you can say to yourself that you accomplished something for the day?

In other words, when all of the big tasks get overwhelming, many people find themselves drawn to accomplishing what they think are short little tasks, even though the work is not important and not urgent. This is a great way to view all of the activities and tasks in your life that are time sucks or time wasters.

Well, it doesn't have to be like that. The more time you carve out for planning and focusing on items that are important and not urgent (box II), the more you will actually get done. It is funny that the more limits you set on yourself, the more you can actually accomplish.

Picking a short task because it seems easy is not the best use of your time. Using this method of planning is not strategic, not efficient, and not effective. It reflects short-term thinking and a distraction mentality.

So how can you grow a business, take care of your clients, and spend 70 to 80 percent of your time marketing your business?

One word: **Delegate!**

Secret 1) No one can do it all, and more importantly, why would you want to?

If you are building a business that will have value, that will allow you and your family to live well, and that eventually will be an asset with financial value, the time to start planning for that is now. The way to do that is to start delegating.

What happens if you don't delegate? The short answer is that you become overwhelmed. When you are overwhelmed, you make poor

> 66 I've learned that if you hire smart people and you trust them, it sets you free. My hardest problem is that I am actually pretty good at a lot of things. I had a hard time letting go.
>
> What I did is I hired different people to take on the roles I loved doing, but I was just a mess, I couldn't do it all. I had small kids at the time. I finally hired my different roles, taking them off me. I would hire a role off me, and I knew that I would want to micromanage that role if I didn't consider first mourning the loss of that activity. I would actually first say, 'I may never do this activity again even though I enjoy it. I'm going to mourn the loss of it so that this new person can take this role and rise into the role and fill it in their own unique way.' I knew I would want people to do it like I did; I could be a control freak. I had to fully let go and mourn the loss of doing this role. I hired people who are specialists in their work and knew that they were going to do it better than me. That was a really big deal: figuring out how to let go and trust other people to do the job better than me."
>
> – Nancy Childs Duarte, Duarte Designs www.duarte.com

choices and bad decisions. Instead of expanding your business, you will grind your business down to nothing. This leads to exhaustion, burnout, and business contraction—the exact opposite of what you want.

Leah Grant, service business marketing expert and new business mentor, identifies business owners who don't delegate as having "Lone Ranger Syndrome." These are business owners who believe that they can do it all. But remember, even the Lone Ranger had a horse and Tonto. So the myth is that the Lone Ranger did it all and did it all alone.

Having "Lone Ranger Syndrome" is overwhelming and exhausting. It leads to going out of business—nothing that anyone wants. Leah tells business owners, "Just because you can do it all, doesn't mean you should." She goes on to instruct business owners that their businesses can only get as big as they are not busy. And if they are doing it all, they are very busy, so how can they grow? Think about it. Where will you put more clients? How will you be able to service them all if you are too busy doing everything else?

Secret 2) You can't afford not to delegate.

The fact of the matter is that many business owners think that they can't afford to delegate, when the truth is they cannot afford not to. Profitability does not come from doing it all yourself—this does not lead to making more money.

The bottom line is that it costs your business when you do not delegate! You are worth more to your business doing income-generating activities that cannot be delegated than doing activities that can be shared with the people you hire. Remember, if you spend 75 percent of your time marketing, then all of the other tasks, chores, and activities that must be done will have to be done by others.

Secret 3) Keep marketing and delegate all the rest.

What do you delegate? What do you keep on your plate? Well, it depends on what you do well. Think about the things in which you excel. Then ask yourself: What do you bring to your business that no employee can or will?

For most businesses, the owner is also the rainmaker—the one who brings in clients by building relationships with prospects until they feel comfortable enough to start doing business with you and your company. Remember, this is how we defined marketing—and marketing is one of the MOST important tasks you can do to grow

> **"**I spend a lot of time up front talking about my expectations of how I delegate because my goal is to delegate with authority, not just delegate a task. I intentionally don't want people on my team that I have to delegate a task to because to delegate a task means you have to say, 'Step one, step two, step three.' And I don't want that. I want to be able to say, 'Here is the thing I need. I need a handout for this presentation,' or 'I need a new updated order form,' or 'I need a spreadsheet on my marketing strategy for the year that all of us can look at.' I share with them the vision of it and then allow them to create it. I really delegate from that perspective because then I'm delegating authority or empowerment, and I find that I get inspired people who want to do their best work for me."
>
> — Ann Evanston of Warrior-Preneur, www.warrior-preneur.comm

your business. So it follows that business owners should be delegating everything BUT the marketing.

When many business owners hear this, they often moan and groan. Many think that they started their businesses to perform a service or provide some sort of product for their clients or customers, and they would prefer to delegate the marketing and keep the task of taking care of their clients.

While this is understandable, this is not the way to grow a business that will have a financial value in the long term for most small- to medium-sized businesses. If you prefer to work with clients over marketing, planning and running a business, then, perhaps, business ownership is not for you. Perhaps, being an employee is a better route for you professionally.

If, after examining what you are doing and why are you doing it, you still want to be an entrepreneur, then you have to recognize that most of your prospects will prefer to talk to you when deciding whether or not to use you and your company as their service or product supplier. You are the story, you are the brand, and you are the one they want to connect with—this is marketing, this is being the rainmaker.

Some business owners find a partner to be the best way to grow their businesses, but until that happens, or if this is not the right route

66 It has been a challenging business learning curve in the past few years—so much of the business world has changed with the advent of social marketing. Just trying to keep up is grueling. There never seems to be a moment when a business owner should not be attending to some facet of social-media networking. LinkedIn business groups, Facebook connections are but a few of the overwhelming options available to business owners today. But keeping up on these forums limits the time and attention needed to deal with the day-to-day running of a business.

To solve this problem, I found it pays to hire young, 23-year-old help. They are the perfect age, and they have the most up-to-date information and knowledge about social-media networking. For them, there is no learning curve. They come completely aware of the latest technological advances. Once they understand the products or services you are offering, they can plug this into the system and get instant results. I have found great success hiring either part-time or virtual help in this age segment to help me with my social-media networking strategy.

I couldn't possibly run a business and also keep track of the innovations in technology. These young professionals are a blessing."
– Karen Korman/President, Marketing Action Xecutives, Inc.
www.seeandbesafe.com

for you, then your only choice is to delegate many of the other aspects of running your business. All the tasks that need to get done, but are not about bringing in new business, can and should be delegated to someone else. Period.

When I tell business owners this, I frequently get push back. They don't like the idea of delegating. They mistakenly believe that they give up control of their businesses by delegating tasks. I understand this way of thinking, but it is not true. In fact, by delegating the tasks that need to be done, but not necessarily done by you, you actually get more control of your business. You will have more time to make decisions and strategically solve the inevitable problems that arise from the normal course of doing business—and you will no longer be overworked and overwhelmed by the hundreds of tasks that need to get done.

> 66 One thing working with a VA has done for me is it buys me time."
>
> — Alicia Dunams, Bestseller in a Weekend, www.bestsellerinaweekend.com

HOW TO DELEGATE

After you accept that delegating is the only right solution for business growth, the next issue to look at is how you should go about delegating—especially on a limited budget with limited resources. Frankly, all companies, large and small, have a limited number of re-sources. Even the largest multi-national companies have limits placed on their resources. I am defining resources as employees, finances, and time. No matter the size of your company, there are still only 24 hours in a day, so that resource is limited for everyone. The larger the company, most likely, the larger the debt and shareholder responsibilities that place limits on what can be done and by whom. So size, in this case, does not matter. Limits exist for all companies. Thinking that limits only affect you and your business is a myth that many small-to-medium-sized business owners tell themselves as an excuse.

In the Action Items for this chapter, you will find the steps to take to start delegating and get your life and business back on track.

Delegating is not a simple or easy chore to put together, but I promise it will yield huge results for growing your business. If you spend the time doing this wisely, then, delegating will be done with less disruption to the business.

66 Early on with delegating, it allowed me to spend the time on marketing. You always hear from new business owners and solopreneurs, 'I just don't have time. I just don't have time. I just don't have time.' Well, if you delegate some stuff for five hours a week, that's an hour a day that you could market and have a marketing strategy and a marketing plan that will help get you off that financial rollercoaster."

– Ann Evanston of Warrior-Preneur, www.warrior-preneur.com

ACTION ITEMS:

1) **Make a list.** This list would include tasks, chores, and projects. All of them. For the sake of this exercise, I will refer to them as tasks, but it includes everything. Use an Excel spreadsheet and lay it all out. Use one column for daily activities, another for weekly, another for monthly, and one for quarterly.

2) **Identify the goal of each task.** Make a note by each task, stating what results you expect. In other words, why do these tasks need to get done? What are you hoping to accomplish or achieve with these tasks? You will use this list to help you figure out who is best to delegate each task to and to communicate with them what needs to be done and why.

3) **Prioritize your list.** Ask yourself:

- Which ones are the most important tasks for you? Prioritize. If you can't narrow them down in order, at least note which are the five most important ones, then the next five, and the next. Your tasks will then be batched by importance to you.
- What tasks can be done be someone else?
- Which tasks energize you? Be honest.
- Which tasks drain you? Be very honest.
- Which tasks take you the most amount of time?
- Which tasks take you the least amount of time?
- Which ones are you able to hire and train someone else to do? Don't focus on the time it takes to train someone at this point. Just indicate which ones you can hire/train someone to do.

4) **Employee or Contract Position.** Next, you are ready to think about who you want to delegate your tasks to. Do you want to hire an employee? Or hire an outside professional on a contract basis? There are pros and cons to each. Neither is the correct choice for any one business or industry. Things to consider:

- Having an employee allows you to delegate a lot of tasks, but there are financial and legal considerations for taking on an employee.

> **"**In the past when I've worked with an executive assistant, I found that I ended up doing the work because I wasn't organized in the right fashion. I was not giving her work. I felt that it could drive my team crazy if I am not communicating and giving people specific instructions."
>
> – Alicia Dunams, Bestseller in a Weekend,
> www.bestsellerinaweekend.com

- Hiring by the job, or on a contract basis, can be the right way to begin, but as you grow, hiring many different professionals and managing them can get overwhelming without planning and foresight. When delegating any task, personal or professional, think out what needs to be done and why, and then communicate this with the person you hired—this is a great use for the lists you made in steps 1 and 2. Just giving a list of tasks that need to be done without more information can result in employees/contract hires failing to understand what they are doing and why. This can lead to mistakes. If you are clear on what you want done and what results you are looking for, then it will save you time and headaches down the road.

- A great way to find people to delegate to is to ask your prospects and other business professionals you know for their recommendations. I suggest you use one-on-one meetings with people to not only learn about their businesses and to share about yours, but also to ask for their help. Asking for names of people you can delegate to is a great way to engage people in your success. And engagement with people means building relationships—the very definition of marketing. What better way to build your business than to ask clients and prospects for help?

- Be careful about delegating any task to anyone. Get clear on what needs to be done and then find the right person—don't settle just for a warm body. Delegating to the wrong person will be as overwhelming or more as doing it all yourself.

Delegating is a long-run activity. In the short term, it takes time and thought to train someone to do the task the way you want them done. The payoff from the successful delegation is more time for you to grow your business, doing activities that you have strategically identified as important and valuable to both you and your business.

66 I found that when you hire people because you really, really like them, if you don't set some curb boundaries right from the get-go, it can get messy quickly. And when you have to say, 'No, that was incorrect,' or 'No, this is why the way you handled that situation is a problem,' the friendship can get in the way. Whereas, if you hire somebody on a professional level and you have professional boundaries and professional expectations, they expect that that's going to come up and that you're going to coach them through that. Friendship sometimes can muddy that water. I once hired somebody who I knew was in need and thought this is just a great chance for this person to help them make some money, but they didn't want to do the work, which it was an eye-opener for me. I'm like, 'Well, no wonder you're broke. You don't want to do the work.' So I just learned that it's better to separate that caretaker heart part of me in making those decisions and build really great business relationships with people who are lasting and trustworthy, and have that level of loyalty for my team."

– Ann Evanston of Warrior-Preneur, www.warrior-preneur.com

Fortune is in the Follow-Up®:

The art of delegating takes practice. In the long run, delegating will be one of the best things you have ever done to improve the quality of your life as a business owner. Don't get discouraged if your first efforts at delegating are not smooth and easy. This is too important a POWER strategy to ignore.

HOW TO FIND THE FORTUNE IN YOUR FOLLOW-UP

A follow-up system that connects you to your prospects consistently and meaningfully will make the difference between "knowing someone" and doing business with them.

MARKETING IS NOT THE SAME AS ADVERTISING

Let's talk about marketing strategies that go into your marketing plan. When I say marketing, what comes to mind? Many people think of advertising. However, advertising is just one of many marketing strategies, and frequently it is not the right strategy to use.

CJ Hayden writes about six marketing strategies in her book, *Get Clients Now,* and lists them in order of their effectiveness: 1: direct contact/follow-up, 2: networking/referral building, 3: public speaking, 4: writing/PR, 5: promotional events, and 6: advertising.

Interestingly, follow-up, at the top of the Hayden's list, is most effective and is usually the least costly. And advertising, which is what many people think of as "marketing," is listed as least effective, and it is frequently the most expensive.

Many of my clients come to me with the mistaken belief that if they just had a lot of money in their marketing budgets, they could grow their businesses, when in reality, they have the tools at their disposal for just the price of a phone call. This leads to my third POWER strategy: **There is a fortune in your follow-up IF you follow-up with your prospects and clients consistently and meaningfully.** I recommend that everyone add follow-up as a strategy to their marketing plans—this means planning for following up by creating a follow-up strategy and that you schedule every event where you'll add new people in your calendar.

THE DEFINITION OF FOLLOW-UP

According to The Free Dictionary.com site, the definition of follow-up is:

1. The act or an instance of following up, as to further an end or review new developments: *The follow-up is often as important as the initial contact in gaining new clients.*

2. One that follows so as to further an end or increase effectiveness: *The software was a successful follow-up to the original product.*

While these definitions are fine, I think the two examples are fabulous. The first example explains why businesses use follow-up in their marketing plans—because follow-up is critical to gaining clients.

A great marketing strategy for business professionals to use is attending networking events, either formal or informal. Using this strategy involves investing time, energy, and sometimes money. But, all too frequently, business owners complain that they are not getting enough business from the networking events they attend. What they are missing is the follow-up. This is THE key ingredient for successful prospect-to-client conversion. The higher the price point of your goods or services, the more this is true.

Finding new prospects with whom to build relationships is an important part of growing a business, but too often, I see business owners spend all their marketing efforts on reaching new people, with little or no effort spent to work on the new people they meet. In other words, after you meet someone, what is next?

Let's say networking is a strategy in your marketing plan. You have identified the events that your target market attends, and you commit to being there regularly. You show up and meet a few people who are either your target market OR they work with your target market. You exchange business cards and leave on a happy note. When you get back to your office, you might add their contact information into your database system (or not). But then what? For most people, nothing else happens.

Now if you understand the basics of how to grow a business, you try contacting them, but let's say they don't respond. What do you do next? Again, if you are like most people, the simple answer is nothing. Nothing more happens, and each name becomes one of a long list of people in your database system, and each person's business card sits in a stack somewhere in your office, doing nothing for you. The next month, you attend the same networking event, collect even more cards, and repeat the cycle all over again.

"I started my Silpada Designs jewelry business on the fast track, making every effort to do things right. I held parties, asked everyone at the party to host a show, and then always did customer-care calls

after the jewelry was received to make sure my customers were happy with everything. I made the follow-up phone calls religiously for my first year. This consistency helped me to have phenomenal sales volume, finishing the sales year in the top 100 Silpada reps in the country for personal sales. As I started getting busy with more parties and with family life and activities, sometimes the follow-up calls would slip. Last fall, I got so busy, that I just didn't get around to calling. I wondered if it even mattered. Did my customers really care that I called?

The answer to that question hit me this year. At every party in the fall, when I asked my customers if they'd like to host a party, they agreed and threw out a time a few months in the future. I wrote that down on their order forms and then moved on to the next customer. This is where I dropped the ball. I placed the order, and they received their jewelry, but I never called to check in. I left my customers hanging. I wasn't reinforcing our relationship by doing my follow-up. I should have been contacting each customer to ask how they liked the jewelry and reiterate how much I'd like to help them earn free jewelry by hosting a jewelry party.

After the holidays, I got back to business and started booking parties for the new year. After a few weeks of randomly calling prospective hostesses, I wasn't getting much traction. I wondered where the magic was. I attended our Silpada team meeting, and Heidi was speaking on the topic of "How to Make Networking Work for You." Heidi touched on many aspects of meeting people, marketing yourself, and creating a networking strategy. She emphasized that the key to all of these things is the follow-up. She insisted that after attending any networking event, you have to schedule time the next day to do the follow-up. I started thinking about the booking woes I was having, and it became clear that my follow-up skills were lacking.

I really had to schedule my follow-up in my calendar. This is when

I realized that follow-up helps build a relationship—which is a key component in marketing.

I decided to go back to basics. I went through last fall's customer order forms and wrote down everyone who had shown an interest in hosting a party. I made a list of names, phone numbers, and email addresses. Then I looked at my calendar and planned when I would call to follow-up with each one. I started dialing and left a lot of voice mails. I made notes in my database and scheduled the next call for a couple days later. When a voice mail wasn't getting a response, I sent an email. I was persistent and methodical with my follow-up. Of course, I got some no's, but more importantly I got some yeses!

The parties, a key strategy for marketing my business, started to come back. However, this time, things are different. Now, after a party, I schedule to follow-up with all my customers on their purchases. I enter the notes into my calendar right away so I know when I need to follow-up with new and potential party hostesses. When I meet someone at a party, I ask when a good time to call is, and I make sure to follow-up when I say I will.

I have been able to increase my party schedule back up to my standard of 5 or 6 a month. I am building stronger relationships with my clientele, so that they will want to do business with me in the future.

People like to do business with people they know. Simple follow-up helps build relationships so that down the road, when a client is ready, they will give you the business and more importantly, refer you to their friends. I am happy to say that at the end of this quarter, I am at number 72 in the country for personal sales. I hope to see that number climb to the top 50 as I continue to build relationships with my customers through good follow-up."

~ Liz Brockman, Independent Silpada Designs Representative, Sterling Silver Jewelry, www.mysilpada.com/liz.brockman

EFFECTIVE FOLLOW-UP

The message has gotten out that in order to grow a business, you need to have a list of prospects and market to that list, but too often, people forget that growing the list is a means to an end. Just growing the list will do nothing for your business unless you work your list. More on that later, let's get back to our networking business-person example.

Follow-up done once is lame and ineffective. But let's take another look at the second definition of follow-up from earlier in this chapter: "One that follows so as to further an end or increase effectiveness."

As I mentioned in Chapter One, one of my favorite words is effective. My second favorite word is productive, as in yielding favorable results, creating constructive outcomes, producing wealth or value. So any effort or task that you are doing to grow your business must be effective or productive, and ideally both!

If something is neither productive nor effective, why are you doing it? What is productive or effective about collecting business

PRODUCTIVE:
1. Producing or capable of producing.
2. Producing abundantly; fertile.
3. Yielding favorable or useful results; constructive.
4. Economics of or involved in the creation of goods and services to produce wealth or value.
5. Effective in achieving specified results

http://www.thefreedictionary.com/productive

cards if they do nothing but collect dust in your office? The answer is obviously nothing. Holding someone's business card does not make a business relationship!

Using networking as a marketing strategy without follow-up is neither productive nor effective. In fact, doing ANY marketing that does not involve follow-up is not productive and is not effective. Sometimes you may yield a single sale, but only now and then. However, if you want to build a business, then your marketing plan must have follow-up as a strategy in place, front and center.

Bottom line: you have two options if you spend time, energy, and/or money to market your business without a follow-up plan in place. Either you can stop marketing altogether, OR you can add a follow-up strategy to your marketing plan and be more productive and more effective, thereby increasing your bottom line.

FOLLOW-UP BARRIERS

Take a few minutes right now and write down the top five reasons you are not doing the follow-up that you know will make a difference to grow your business.

1) _____

2) _____

3) _____

4) _____

5) _____

The number one response from business professionals who do this exercise is lack of time. They believe that they don't have enough time to add follow-up to their marketing plans. Is this you? Well, let's explore this assumption.

PRIORITIES

Frankly, we all have enough time to do everything that is important to us. The hard part is to figure out what is important to us. How you spend your time is a way of identifying what is important to you. If you spend your time watching TV, then that is one of your priorities. If you spend your time reading books, then that is one of your priorities. If you spend your time being your own bookkeeper or webmaster, then those are your priorities. Or if you spend your time marketing your business and serving your clients, then these are your priorities. So what will it be?

EXERCISE: WHAT ARE YOUR PRIORITIES?

Take a few minutes to list how you are spending your time.

	MON	TUES	WED	THUR
6AM				
7AM				
8AM				
9AM				
10AM				
11AM				
12PM				
1PM				
2PM				
3PM				
4PM				
5PM				
6PM				
7PM				

	MON	TUES	WED	THUR
8PM				
9PM				
10PM				

	FRI	SAT	SUN
6AM			
7AM			
8AM			
9AM			
10AM			
11AM			
12PM			
1PM			
2PM			
3PM			
4PM			
5PM			
6PM			
7PM			
8PM			
9PM			
10PM			

If you cannot reconstruct your last seven days, keep track of the next seven and then take a look at how you are spending your time.

After looking at the completed chart, answer the follow questions:

1) Which of your activities are generating income?

2) Which of your activities will lead to increased business?

3) Which of your activities are just time sucks that take you away from growing your business and making profit?

4) What activities help you to rest, relax, and renew?

5) Defined by how you spend your time, what are your priorities?

There are a limited number of hours in a day, and that will not change. But how you spend your time can change. We all make conscious and unconscious choices, and the key part of being successful is to make sure that your choices affect your priorities positively. If you are not being conscious in your choices, then most likely you are allowing your choices to impact your priorities negatively.

In my four-part time-management program, I have participants identify their priorities, list all of the activities, projects, and tasks they do, and then clear away those that prevent them from achieving their priorities.

Over the years, I have noticed that most people know what it is they should be doing to grow their businesses, but they allow excuses to prevent them from moving forward—like the excuse of not having the time to do the follow-up they know they should be doing.

FOLLOW-UP CHALLENGE

Here is a challenge: What do you think would happen if you added the following to your to-do list: calling and connecting with five prospects and/or clients weekly? You would increase your sales immediately. I once gave a group of direct marketing consultants the challenge to contact three prospects a week for three months for follow-up. Guess what happened? They grew their businesses because of the follow-up calls and contact—some doubled their businesses in that short time, most grew at a more reasonable rate. Either way, how would it feel if you could grow your business this quarter by a third, just by making contact with three prospects a week for the next three months, and all for the cost of a phone call?

You may be thinking, *when do I have the time to do this?* But before we get into making the time, I want you to think about what contacting prospects and current clients will do to grow your business.

Here is one of my follow-up success stories.

During a speaking presentation, I collected attendees' business cards for a drawing at the event and then added their contact information to my database for the purposes of follow-up and my business-building newsletter.

A few weeks after my presentations, I spent time contacting some of the attendees to see what impact my presentation had on their business practices and to offer them a spot in an upcoming program. Usually, I have a pretty good success rate for filling program seats in this way. Little did I know that by making one call to one person, I would fill up a program that I wasn't even offering at the time!

Here is what happened: I called a real estate agent, who had attended a free one-hour presentation I had given on sales tips, to let her know about an upcoming program I had on time management. She quickly stated that she was interested in attending a four or five session program that presented the material in a workshop format. Since I had done this program before, it was an easy request to me. So I agreed, and I asked her to help market it to the other agents in her office. We agreed on a price per agent, she marketed it, and suddenly I had a full class of real estate agents (one of my target markets) all interested in learning how to be more effective at marketing themselves. I have expanded it to other real estate offices in the area, too! How did this happen? I made the follow-up phone call.

What happens when you talk directly to a prospect? You are building a relationship. We know people do business with people with whom they have a relationship. How will your prospects develop a relationship with you if you do not have any contact with them? How will they get to know, like, and trust you if the only connection you have with them is the one time you met them and then added their name to your database and their business card to your card file? The answer is they won't. Let's change that now.

BUILDING A RELATIONSHIP

In the previous chapter, I talked about delegating. I hope that you used the action items assignment to figure out what tasks to delegate and what tasks to keep on your to-do list. One task that must stay on your list is connecting with your prospects and clients—and not just when you are working with them. Relationship building is critical, and follow-up is the way to do this.

There are several ways to approach adding follow-up to your marketing plan. The first is to target new prospects, and the second is to target past clients. In the bonus chapter, **The Power of Networking: 5 Simple Strategies to Make Money,** I explain how to add networking as a strategy to your marketing plan to target new prospects. For now, let's focus on targeting your past clients. These are the people with whom you have done business in the past, but no longer have a current engagement.

Your past clients are a great market to target. They already know, like, and trust you—they showed you that by doing business with you

> **❝** I really believe in trying to connect with everybody if I can, because, and it's part of what I teach my clients and my own business, I firmly believe that people who only follow-up because they think somebody's going to buy have completely missed the point. Because I believe in creating relationships that become referral sources. As a matter of fact, my first Facebook client who ended up being a $6,500-a-month client for a year was through a referral.
>
> I'm amazed at how many people I have followed up with, and they have then written a blog about me and I can use that blog. They haven't bought from me. I have a woman who I've known for three years who hasn't bought from me, but she writes blogs about me all the time. And those blogs become press that I can use to create new business. So I'm a big believer in trying to connect with every person in terms of that because you never know where the opportunities are."
>
> – Ann Evanston of Warrior-Preneur, www.warrior-preneur.com

in the past. But for some reason, they are no longer doing business with you. The odds are that they stopped buying from you because they got out of the habit of thinking of you when they need more of what you offer.

REMIND YOUR PAST CLIENTS

As humans, we are creatures of habit, and marketing your business sometimes involves helping your past clients get back into the habit of coming to you to buy your goods and services. Your follow-up is to remind them that you are still here and able to help them.

I have a client who is a talented acupuncturist. She has great skills in healing clients who come to her for all sorts of discomfort and illnesses. When they are healed, they thank her and end their treatments. But then what happens when inevitably they get hurt or fall ill again? Do they always think of going back? Some will, but many might forget, and this is where conversations, continued contact, and regular engagement during the time they are well comes into play. In other words, follow-up!

Of course, we want our past clients to always remember us when they need us again, but in this day and age of so much information overload, many of our clients forget who we are when we are not front and center in their lives. What is the solution? To use follow-up strategies that offer meaningful connections.

MEANINGFUL CONNECTIONS

Understanding what a meaningful connection with your prospects is will make the difference between growing your business with repeat customers or not.

Meaningful

a : having a MEANING or purpose
b : full of MEANING : SIGNIFICANT
http://www.merriam-webster.com/ dictionary/ meaningful

The key element to a meaningful connection is that it has to be significant to your prospects—not necessarily to you. When you contact a prospect, the information you share with them has to be of benefit and provide value to them. So if you choose to send out a newsletter (electronic or hard) as a strategy in your marketing plan, you must make sure that it provides value to your prospects and clients and is not just an infomercial about you and your company. Otherwise, it is not a meaningful connection for them, and your prospects and clients will unsubscribe from your mailing list.

EDUCATION-BASED MARKETING

Another way to look at this is to start using what is called education-based marketing for your marketing plan. Education-based marketing educates your prospects and clients by sharing information that they will find valuable, as opposed to constantly pitching to them. IF you have done a good job at educating your prospects by showing them that you understand and know their pain points, and IF you can demonstrate your value as a solution provider, then your prospects will want to hire you and pay you.

Here are some wonderful examples of education-based marketing from Christine Comaford, CEO of business accelerator Mighty Ventures and the author of the best-selling book Rules for Renegades, showing the difference between making a pitch at prospects and showing your value to them.

http://www.businessweek.com/smallbiz/content/oct2007/sb2007108_051696.htm

"To drive my point home about the power of education-based marketing, let's review three ineffective education-based marketing approaches, along with much more effective approaches.

Business: Real Estate Agency

Ineffective offer: Let me teach you why you should list your house with me.

Effective offer: Let me teach you the five mistakes everyone makes when selling a house. No matter who you list with, you'll need to know these things.

Business: Financial Planner

Ineffective offer: I want to come and talk to you about how I can help you plan for a better financial future.

Effective offer: Even if you never do anything with me, I want to make sure you know that there are five critical mistakes everyone makes in trying to accumulate wealth.

Business: Technology Services Company

Ineffective offer: Let me tell you how great we are at helping with your IT services.

Effective offer: As part of our effort to build better relationships in the business community, we offer a free white paper entitled "Six ways to dramatically increase productivity using your current technology."

Using meaningful, education-based marketing, you will show your past clients (and prospects) that you know their pain points and are the solution to their problems. You will demonstrate your value to them as a service provider or product supplier. The key is to make sure what you provide is meaningful to them.

I highly recommend that all your marketing tools, no matter which strategies you employ, whether you are talking to new prospects or past clients, use an education-based format as your underlying strategy.

THE SALES PROCESS

In order to better understand how and why follow-up is effective, let's talk briefly about the sales process.

"The only purpose of attending a live event is to get exposure, meet people, and build a relationship. If you try to make a sale on the spot, you are making a big mistake. You must build a relationship first. You can't do that if you see people only once and never follow-up with them."
- Biba F. Pédron, Marketing Consultant, founder of Biba4Network

People don't buy when you want them to buy; they buy when they are ready. And they buy from someone with whom they feel a connection. The purpose of following up is to be that person they feel connected to and be there when they are ready to buy. If you have been consistent and meaningful (think education-based marketing) with your follow-up, then when your prospects are ready to take action, you will get the sale.

Your task is to be there in their minds until they are ready. It is your job to remind them who you are and what you provide for them.

Marketing consultants used to tell business owners that it takes 7 contacts to convert a prospect to being a client. Well, that has changed. A slower economy has made everyone more cautious in their purchases and elongated the process. Instead of 7 contacts, think 12 to 15 contacts before you can reasonably think that a prospect would consider doing business with you. For some industries, it might be closer to 20 contacts.

If you use a monthly newsletter as a strategy in your marketing plan and that is the only contact you have with your database, then you are talking about at least a year's worth of newsletters before any of your prospects will even consider doing business with you—not very effective and not very productive.

Don't get me wrong, I am a big believer in newsletters, as long as they are informational, educational, and valuable to your prospects. I think a newsletter can be a wonderful, inexpensive way to connect with your prospects as a tool for follow-up; however, it is not very effective by itself. Newsletters work best in concert with other follow-up tools and techniques that shorten the time it takes to get in the 12 to 15 contacts that you need to raise your prospect-to-client conversion rate. And of course, the content of your newsletter must be educational to your clients and not just a sales pitch.

It is not your prospect's job to remember you when they need your products or services. One of my pet peeves is when people hand me their business cards, unasked for, and then assume that I will keep it until the day comes when I need to contact them for their goods or services.

Sorry, but that will not be happening. I don't know about you, but I am on information overload most of the time these days. Sometimes, I can barely remember all of the information that is critical to me and my business. There is no way that I will remember someone who provides goods or services that I might need at some time in the future. Where would I put their business cards so that I might find it again months or even years down the road when I finally do need it?

If you want to do business with someone, don't force your business card on them; instead, ask them for their cards and ask permission to add them to your mailing list. Then make sure what you send to them is educational, valuable, and meaningful to them (not you). Keep in contact with them using other tools and techniques, as well (see the Action Items at the end of this chapter). When they are ready to buy, they will remember you because you have been developing a relationship with them with your meaningful education-based marketing strategy.

WHAT HOLDS YOU BACK FROM ADDING FOLLOW-UP TO YOUR MARKETING PLAN?

This is the $64,000 question! Why don't you do the follow-up you know you should be doing with every lead and referral and contact that comes your way? What prevents you from making that connection? What prevents you from letting your prospects know that you exist, that you can solve their problems? What stops you from asking for their business?

Go back to the exercise you did earlier in this chapter. If you listed "not enough time" as one of the reasons that prevents you from following up, then reread the first part of this chapter. What else is on your list that is in your way for adding follow-up to your routine? If you drill down deep enough at the other excuses on your list, you will see that fear is most likely standing in your way. Usually, it is fear of appearing too pushy and/or fear of being rejected.

Most business owners don't really have a solid approach to follow-up, and so they don't explore their options. Instead, they give in to their fears and allow fear to be their main follow-up system operator. Is this you? If so, then you are in good company.

There are thousands and thousands of business owners leaving thousands of millions of dollars worth of business on the table, all because they are not following up with prospects. The good news, though, is that most likely your competitors are also

> "Follow-up is the name of the game for my business. My follow-up strategy is to send my prospects cards from my company and then follow-up with a phone call if I do not hear from them first. I have a turnkey business called SendOutCards, which is very similar to having your own franchise, but with a very low start-up cost.
>
> At a local networking event, I met a woman who sells brick-and-mortar franchises, most of which are over $50,000 to purchase. When asked about lower-priced franchises she has to offer people in our troubled economy, for under $500, she couldn't think of anything. I told her that it cost me less than $500 to start my business and that piqued her interest. We exchanged contact information, and I followed up with her. When we got together and showed her the full line of services and products, she loved it! So much so, she bought her own SOC 'franchise,' and went on to sell it to others.
>
> But here's the coolest part—she sold a SendOutCards 'franchise' to a woman, who then sold a 'franchise' to another woman, who ended up being my most successful team member. I call her my 'Thoroughbred Race Horse.' This woman has brought in so many customers and sold so many franchises, that she is a key component of my current success. Had I not pursued the woman who sold traditional franchises at the networking event, I would never have met my 'Thoroughbred.'"
>
> – Kim Hunter, Independent Distributor of SendOutCards.

not following up with their prospects and past clients, either. This means you have the opportunity to differentiate yourself and get more clients just by adding a follow-up strategy to your marketing plan.

FEARS

Let's examine what you are afraid of if you are allowing your fears to get in the way of conducting and growing your business. When I ask business owners what they are most afraid of when it comes to follow-up, they say, "I don't want to appear too pushy or aggressive," or "I fear being rejected."

One of my children once came home from school and told me that a friend was moving out of the area. As a real estate agent, this was music to my ears. But I did not know the family at all—nada, zip, not a bit. So I had to make a connection. I had to pick up the phone and let them know I could help them. It was not easy to do; in fact, it was downright hard. I spent some time looking at and willing the phone to ring, but that didn't work. So I found the school directory and called them.

Now this was a lukewarm call at best, just one step away from being a cold call. While our boys were in school together and had known each other for a few months, as parents, we had never met. Calling them felt awkward and difficult. To make matters worse, I was new in the real estate business and felt insecure about approaching them. I was also competing with agents in the area who had branded themselves very successfully. In fact, in our town, there was one very successful agent who had built her brand such that anyone buying or selling would at least consult with her. This made it very difficult for other agents to get business, much less for someone new to the area and the industry.

I did it. I made the phone call and got the listing. But the story does not end there. That one listing led to me receiving 11 more real estate transactions in that town. Yes, 11 closed deals came from that one phone call.

Was it hard? Yes, it was. Was I afraid of how I would be perceived? Of course I was. Did I worry about being rejected? Yes, I worried every step along the way. But more important, did I let it stop me? No, I did not!

What connections could you make that will lead to 11 closed deals? What opportunities are you missing because you are allowing fear and doubt to be more important than getting more business?

The difference between those who are successful and those who are not is not the absence of fear, but rather how each deals with their fears. Those who are stuck and not moving up the income ladder allow their fears to rule their businesses. Many business owners are not playing the win-at-business game, but rather they are playing the not-to-lose business game. (More about the playing to-win versus playing the not-to-lose game will be discussed in Chapter Five, **Why Mindset Matters**.) They are allowing their fears to prevent them from making connections, starting the sales process, continuing to contact their prospects and past clients, using meaningful follow-up, and then asking for the business.

Those who are successful in business have not banished their fears; they have not risen above them. Frequently, they have fears, too. But they are not allowing their fears to be in charge of growing their businesses. They are not allowing their fears to interfere with making money.

"Courage is not the absence of fear. It is the ability to take action while feeling afraid."

C.J. Hayden, *Get Clients Now,* 2nd Edition, Page 108.

This is a headline, people! Think about it. If you are waiting for your fears to go away to start doing all of the wonderful and

❝Follow-up can seem like chasing someone and can be discouraging if it seems as if it doesn't make a difference. I've had a number of prospects whom I've 'chased' for many months, and just on the verge of giving up, I've made one more contact. Frequently, this last attempt to connect nets me the response, 'I'm so glad you called. Something just happened which made me think of you. Let's talk.'

In order to make sure I don't let any potentials fall off the radar, I use a pretty detailed tracking system, patched together from several different bits of software. I link every phone call, e-mail, and contact information for each prospect, so I can glance back and see our contact history and any pertinent facts. I also use a master tracking spreadsheet, with all current prospects displayed, along with any relevant information from our discussions. Most important, I have a column showing our last contact. This allows me to quickly glance at my master list and know when it's time to reach out and connect again.

The one big lesson I've learned is never to assume they're just not interested because they haven't responded to my e-mails or calls; I don't give up until they tell me they're not interested! There are many who just don't respond, but when the time is right, things click and we move forward. Sometimes I'll even say, "I hope I'm not being a pest,' and they'll frequently respond to that saying, 'Oh, no, I appreciate your checking in and keeping me on your radar.'"

— Beth Weisberg, workplace essentials, coaching and training for a better workplace powerful business strategies that you have heard about, know about, and want to implement, then I have good news and bad news.

The bad news is that fears will never go away completely for many people. For most, though, fears can be significantly reduced. So if you are waiting for that day when you are not at all afraid of how you will be seen, perceived, or rejected when contacting your prospects, that day may never come.

However, the good news is that it gets easier over time. And the more you do it, the more you will start having successful outcomes. Now, not all of your contacts will start to do business with you, but as you start to engage in more **meaningful** interactions, you will start to be more **effective.** The more effective you become, the more confidence you will have and exude, which will lead to better quality interactions with your prospects and clients. This will lead to a lessening of your fears and much more business.

One last note, if your fears of being too pushy or aggressive are preventing you from following up with prospects and clients, know that in my years of experience of working with business owners, the people with these fears are rarely, if ever, too aggressive or pushy. People with these fears are, more often than not, allowing their fears to prevent them from engaging with their prospects. Most likely, if you have these fears, you are being insecure and not seeing yourself and what you have to offer as valuable to your prospects. Most of the time, the people who are too pushy and aggressive never worry about it. So if this is you, stop allowing this fear to prevent you from connecting with your prospects and clients.

ACTION ITEMS:

7 TECHNIQUES OF EFFECTIVE FOLLOW-UP:

1. **Systematize.** In order to make follow-up work, you must use a system. Systematizing is a way of making your life easier by not having to reinvent what you are doing each time you repeat a task or process that you do on a regular basis. Systematizing is a way of leveraging your time—and the more you can systematize, the more you can delegate your tasks to others. You begin systematizing by keeping track of every process that you repeat during the sales and follow-up process. It takes a little bit more time at first, but by setting up systems, you end up winning in the long term. Knowing what you are to do with prospects means you will be much more likely to actually engage with them, thereby creating relationships that will lead to more business.

2. **Top-Notch Database System.** You will need a top-notch database system—one that works great for you in your industry. It does not have to be the fanciest system with all the latest bells and whistles. It does have to be able to do what you need it to do. If you want to track your interactions with prospects, then this should be a feature in the system you choose. If you want to be able to share the data with your virtual assistant, that should be a feature. If you want your system to categorize your contacts, look for that feature. If you want it to work with a calendar system, populating your contacts' information when you schedule appointments or meetings, the ability to do so should be a feature in the system you select. Not sure what you need? Start keeping a list of ideas. Then contact your colleagues, clients, and competitors and pick their brains about what they use and why.

3. Education-Based Marketing. Keep a file (hard or electronic) of articles and information that you write and/or come across from industry e-zines, magazines, newsletters, blogs, etc. This is information that you will share with your prospects and clients in your education-based marketing. You can use this information in your newsletters OR as conversation topics when following up with your prospects and past clients. This is information that, if they knew about it, would help them see the value in hiring you as their [fill in the blank with your profession] expert.

This information demonstrates you as an industry expert or subject matter expert (SME). It needs be informational, educational, and add value to your prospects and clients. You need to think strategically about what your prospects and clients need to know about working with you or hiring an expert in your field. You must use language that will connect with and draw the interest of your prospects and clients, and not just use industry jargon that you and your competitors know and use. Using articles from your industry publications is a great way to start demonstrating your value as an SME, since few, if any, of your prospects and clients are reading your industry journals. The information will be new and fresh to your prospects and clients.

4. Multi-Contact Follow-up System. Make sure you use a multi-contact follow-up system. Remember, if it takes at least 12 to 15 contacts to convert a prospect to a client, then it is important to have a system that uses multiple ways to contact them over a period of time. One email or one newsletter will not convert a prospect into a client. Have a plan that delivers your message to your list on a regular basis—at least once a month, but not more than once a week. Less than once a month is not enough for you to be top of mind, and once a week borders on stalking. Remember, whatever you share must add value to your prospects and clients' lives.

5. Benefits that Sell. Make sure you use language that shows how you and your company will help them—make it a benefit statement to their needs, not to what you offer. AND don't forget to include new programs and services that you have so that they learn how your company can solve their problems and will think of you as the resource in your field that you are.

❝I think that it's important to have that personal touch; to let the person that you're following up with know that it's coming from you. It's not a canned response. It's a phone call. It's a note. It's an email that really does look like it's not a form letter but is bringing out points of a conversation that you all might have had before.

As much as possible, follow-up personally and put a system in place that's manageable. Follow-up needs to be considered marketing, and it needs to be considered as an important part of your business, not just, 'Oh, good grief, I don't have time for that' and let it fall by the wayside.

Follow-up is hard, and it's not easy. And I've even gone so far as to ask people how they would prefer I follow-up. 'Would you prefer a call? Would you prefer email? Would you prefer I connect with you on Facebook? What would you prefer?' And I write that on the back of their cards when they give it to me."

— Sanyika Calloway Boyce of Sanyika Worldwide, http://tvpublicitysecrets.com

6. Personal Touch. Personal touch is better than rote forms. If you use pre-written letters, then find a system in which you can at least deliver your pieces from you and in your handwriting. There are all sorts of wonderful online systems to use, but make sure that your prospects and clients will see it positively. Not sure? Then take a poll. Survey your clients and ask them for their opinions. This is a great way to follow-up *and* engage with them. For more on surveying your prospects and clients, see chapter on **7 Stellar Customer Service Strategies.**

7. The Phone is Your Friend. Don't forget the phone is a fine way to follow-up with prospects—don't call to make a sale, but do call and ask how you can be of service to them. If you end up making a sale, then great, but this is NOT the purpose of your call.

Fortune is in the Follow-Up®:
developing your relationships with people makes money. Don't be afraid to make the connection. What 11 closed deals are waiting for you from just one call? Take the follow-up challenge: Make three follow-up calls a week for the next three months and watch your revenue grow!

BONUS CHAPTER:
THE POWER OF
NETWORKING:
5 SIMPLE STRATEGIES
TO MAKE MONEY

"You can't overestimate the need to plan and prepare. In most of the mistakes I've made, there has been this common theme of inadequate planning beforehand. You really can't over-prepare in business!"
- Chris Corrigan, Australian businessman

Definition of Networking

Networking is: "to interact or engage in informal communication with others for mutual assistance."
from http://www.thefreedictionary.com/network

Networking is a great marketing strategy for most marketing plans since it is about building relationships and making connections—the very definition of marketing (see Chapter One). I am a big fan of networking as a marketing strategy, but it is important that you make sure it fits for you and your business. There are a few industries and target markets where networking will not work; however, they are the exception and not the rule.

For most businesses, networking is a powerful strategy, but there are a few important things to consider before adding it to your marketing plan. In this bonus chapter, we will explore the options further so that when you go to networking events, you will be both effective and productive.

NETWORKING CAN BE DONE INFORMALLY OR FORMALLY.

Informal networking involves casual interactions about your business with people at non-work-related gatherings. This can include sporting events, school events, parties, shopping, etc. —or any activity or event that you are engaged in during which you have an opportunity to connect with a prospect or referral source and share information about you and doing business with you.

Two great examples of informal networking are:

1) When I was an active real estate agent in the Midwest in the 1990's, I found the perfect property for a client while on the tennis court. I was making conversation and mentioned that after the game, I was taking a new client to look for condominiums in a certain neighborhood. In response, one of the other players mentioned that she had a new listing coming on in a few days that might work for my client. Long story short, it was just what we were looking for, and my client ended up buying it. My client thought I was a hero for learning about it before it was on the market.

2) One of my clients sold a room full of window coverings when she overheard two women at Starbucks talking about their next errand to find draperies. She did not start with a sales pitch, but rather told the women that she overheard them and was an expert in that field. She invited them to her showroom around the corner to advise them before they started shopping, so that at the very least, they would know what to look for and what to avoid. This turned into $2,000 sale for her. All it cost her was a cup of coffee.

Both of these examples involve interacting in informal communication with others at informal or non-professional settings. Neither of us expected when we went out to play tennis or get a cup of coffee that we would end up making money while away from work, but that is exactly what happened. It pays to be on the lookout for any opportunity to talk about your business, even in non-business settings.

Formal networking involves getting together for the purpose of meeting other people with similar interests. Sometimes the networking is expressly for meeting new professional contacts to grow your business, and sometimes not. Either way, if your target market were there, it would be a good idea for you to be there, too. And, of course, networking with people who work with your target market is another option. In other words, you don't have to only network with your target market, networking with referral sources is also a great way to grow your business.

CAN ANYONE BE GOOD AT NETWORKING?

Many people have the mistaken notion that only extroverts can be good at networking. If anything, the opposite may be true—introverts have the inside edge on networking. Think about it, extroverts get their energy from being around other people, and introverts get their energy from being by themselves. Neither is better than the other. However, because extroverts like being around people, they approach networking differently than introverts, and this may cause a problem for extroverts when it comes to networking.

Can't tell if you are an introvert or an extrovert? There are all sorts of wonderful tools and assessments available to help you determine your preference. However, one quick-and-easy way is to give yourself an assignment to spend 3 hours alone in your home or office doing a project without interacting with anyone else. If you are fine about this, and get a lot done and then afterwards feel great, most likely you are an introvert. If, however, you spend the first 15 to 20 minutes on this project and then find yourself wanting to call, email, or connect with someone, you are most likely an extrovert.

Smart introverts know that networking usually means being around other people and that, since this can drain them, they need to approach these events with a plan. While extroverts approach networking with confidence and ease, since they get energized from being with people, they usually figure that they can "wing it" without a plan.

What happens when you work on something without a plan? Often, it means that what you want to accomplish does not get done. By approaching networking without a plan or a strategy, extroverts can end up being less successful at it than introverts. The bottom line is that everyone needs a networking strategy if they are going to use networking in their marketing plans. Marketing expert Leah

Grant shares a wonderful concept in which she explains that business owners should: "Think of networking as being like rapid or speed dating. In which two people have a few minutes to determine, 1) if they serve the same target market, 2) if they provide complimentary products, and 3) if they like one another enough to go to the next step. Then one of you must take the next step and ask the other one out on a business date or the prelim work was a waste."

4 QUESTIONS YOU SHOULD ASK AT A NETWORKING EVENT

Here are four questions you should ask people you meet at networking events.

1) How did you get started in your business?
2) How did you name your business?
3) What do you offer to your clients; what do you do for them?

Who is your target market; who do you like to work with? Using this short list of questions will help give you conversation topics—and it will enable you to focus on learning about the person you are talking to, rather than doing the talking yourself. This is good for both introverts and extroverts.

Once you have engaged in conversation with the people you meet, you can see if there is overlap between your businesses and figure out if you want to get together outside of the networking event—where the real work happens.

WHAT TO EXPECT AT NETWORKING EVENTS

Business is not usually done at networking events. Networking is a time to meet other people and to see IF you want to engage in more conversation, getting to know each other well enough to see if you might want to do business. Meeting someone once at a networking event is not usually enough to get to know them, like them, and trust them. This means when you go to networking events, don't go in with the expectation that you will be hired while there—just as you don't plan to hire someone on the spot either.

As stated in **Chapter Three: How to Find the Fortune in Your Follow-up**, understanding how the sales process works is critical. Approaching new people at networking events with the idea that you want them to hire you does not work. We have all had the bad experience in which someone was overly pushy by trying to close a sale before a relationship has been established or having someone not take no for an answer.

PUSHY IS NOT THE SAME AS PITCHING

Over the years, a common theme I've heard from many business owners is that they fear appearing pushy or aggressive when talking to prospects at networking events or otherwise. People who fear being too aggressive rarely are. Too many business people are mistaken when they think that being aggressive and being an advocate for yourself (and your business) is the same thing. If you don't let people know how doing business with you will help them, then you are not doing your job as an entrepreneur. You will not be able to convert prospects into clients, and they will ultimately work with your competitors, who may or may not be as good as you are.

The time you invest to help your prospects get to know, like, and trust you will pay off with increased sales and profits. Rushing the process leads to turning off people, but not participating in the process at all means no growth, no sales, and no profit.

In order to make networking a successful part of your marketing plan, I recommend you develop a strategy. Without one, you

When I was online, I came across a cute acronym that spelled out what none of us want to be known as: A GROSS networker: Getting Really Offensive with Selfish Selling. Don't mistake being pushy or aggressive with making your sales pitch—these behaviors are not the same approaches at all. Although, if done too soon in the sales process, your sales pitch will resemble being pushy. What to do? Learn about the sales process and don't stop making your sales pitch—learn when it fits and when it doesn't.

are much less effective and productive. You will end up wasting your time, energy, and money. Plus, with the free food served at networking events, it could be a great way to gain weight, with little else to show for your efforts. With a strategy, you can use networking to grow your business—and for not that much money, either.

"An enterprising person is one who comes across a pile of scrap metal and sees the making of a wonderful sculpture. An enterprising person is one who drives through an old decrepit part of town and sees a new housing development. An enterprising person is one who sees opportunity in all areas of life," according to Jim Rohm, American entrepreneur, author, and motivational speaker.

NETWORKING IS ABOUT BUILDING RELATIONSHIPS AND ABOUT SEEING OPPORTUNITIES

If you chose to use networking as a strategy in your marketing plan, you can reap large rewards; however, keep in mind that networking does not usually bring in short-term results—it is a strategy to use when you have a longer timeframe in mind.

The good news is that networking does not take a lot of money. Now that there are networking events everywhere that meet at all times of the day, it has become a great way to grow a business on a limited marketing budget. In order to make networking a successful strategy in your marketing plan, you must be able to make the time commitment to show up regularly, pick the right venues, set workable goals, and then follow-up with those you meet.

There are some service business owners I know who have marketing plans that use nothing but networking. They participate in many networking events, employ all of the tips outlined in this chapter and the chapter on follow-up, and make each event work for them.

ACTION ITEMS:
5 STEPS TO BETTER NETWORKING

1) **Target your Networking Events.** Be strategic in choosing which ones you will attend. In order to do this effectively, you will need to know your target market well. Where does your target market hang out? What meetings, organizations, conventions, or conferences do they attend? And don't forget, attending networking events with great referral sources is another terrific way to use networking effectively and productively for growing your business.

2) **Schedule.** Once you determine which networking events you want to attend, schedule when they meet into your calendar for the year. It takes commitment to use networking as a successful marketing strategy: commitment to the group, commitment to show up, commitment to follow-up, and commitment to develop relationships. Showing up once will not have much effect on your business. If you are not able to commit to a group, then don't add them to your list—even if they are the perfect match for your target market.

Once you add the networking events and groups that you commit to in your calendar, don't forget to block out time the next day for your follow-up. For every networking opportunity you attend, make sure that you follow-up the next day with those people you want to get to know better.

3) Set Networking Goals. Set some goals before you attend. Think about why you are there and what you want to accomplish. If your only goal is to get clients, then either don't attend or rethink your goals—remember don't be GROSS. When business owners put together a marketing plan, I like to remind them that there are all sorts of goals to think about. Great networking goals include meeting people with whom you can: connect, have fun, be able to help, be authentic with, be an interested listener, be curious, ask questions, be of service, build rapport, and meet potential clients.

What happens when you have no goals and attend networking events? Well, it is like driving somewhere without a map or GPS. Most likely, you will eventually get to where you are going, but a journey that should only take days could end up taking months or even years.

Bottom line: you want to make sure that you do any and all of the above, along with the goal of meeting three or four people who you want to pursue outside of the networking event. These three or four people would be people with whom you share a similar target market, complimentary products or service, and would like to get to know better.

Distributing your business cards to all the attendees is not an effective strategy. Remember, holding someone's business card does not mean you have a relationship with them. Cultivating three or four meaningful relationships is a much more worthwhile endeavor for a networking event than handing out your business cards to everyone at the event.

If the goals you set for attending networking events are about building relationships versus making sales, you will find the power in networking as a strategy for your marketing plan.

4) Ask Questions. What do you want to say to people when you meet them? This will be determined by the goals you set, but should always involve asking questions, preferably open-ended questions that are designed to help you get to know the people with whom you are talking. Ideally, you have developed an elevator pitch with a unique benefit statement (see **Chapter Four: 7 Stellar Customer Service Strategies**). Remember, a great elevator pitch is not a sales pitch. It is designed to help generate interest in you and what you offer. Ideally, the response to your elevator pitch is, "Please tell me more."

Engaging *with* people is not the same as talking at them. If you want to be effective at networking, focus more on being interested in them, versus being interesting to them. The paradox of listening is that the more interested you are in others, the more they will perceive you as interesting. The art of being a great listener is all about being seen as someone who is truly interested in what other people are saying without being judgmental.

5) Be of Service. Since building relationships is your overall objective when networking, then it is important that you listen and respond to people. Asking them how you may be of service and then following through is a great way to build a relationship with a prospect. If you are able to provide help to them, directly or through someone in your network, you will be able to build a connection with them. Relationship building is not just about how you help someone professionally, it can be about how you help them in other aspects of their lives, as well.

Think about how you feel about people who help you. Are you more or less inclined to remember them, think positively about them, *and* to refer clients to them? If you are like most people, you will think positively about people who help you. So finding how you can help someone else, and not just professionally, will lead to building a relationship, which leads to business. I once had a client hire me after knowing me for several months, and the final tipping point was my sharing with her a recommendation for a housepainter!

Now if you offer to provide something for someone new who you meet while networking, it is critical that you follow through on what you promise. Don't make an offer that you cannot deliver. Make sure that you have the time and resources to make good on what you offer.

When you first meet someone and they are just getting to know you, it is important that you demonstrate to them that you are trustworthy, which shows them that you are dependable. How do you do that? By following through on what you promise to do for them. Otherwise, you can lose your reputation by over promising and under delivering before you have had the chance to really get to know them.

Fortune is in the Follow-Up®:
Don't forget that following up with people you meet while networking is the whole point of attending. It does you no good to meet new people, collect their contact information, and then do nothing with it! Break the habit of not following up.

4

7 STELLAR CUSTOMER SERVICE STRATEGIES

MARKETING MODEL FOR SUCCESS REVISITED

As I mentioned in **Chapter One: How to Define Your Target Market,** one of the business models I use with clients is:

> Great customer service ➔ leads to more referrals ➔ means more business ➔ leads to higher prices ➔ leads to making more $!

The web is full of programs and business coaches selling programs about how to create a 6- or 7-figure business. While I am all for making money, there is really only one way to do it, and that is to continually meet or exceed your clients' expectations so that they continue to do business with you AND refer others to do business with you. This is the model that I have had success with, both as a business owner and a business mentor.

> **"**If you have a good product and world-class customer service, the phone should ring. It should diminish the amount that you have to spend in sales."
>
> – Nancy Duarte Childs of Duarte Design, www.duarte.com

CUSTOMER SERVICE STRATEGY 1: THE NAME OF THE GAME IS TO SERVE YOUR CLIENTS' NEEDS

Let's break it down. How and why did you start your business? Had you been in your industry previously, working for another company? Or did you leave a career in a totally different profession? Either way, now that you own and run a business, you must make sure that you serve your clients' needs and not just your dreams of running your own business and calling your own shots. Many business owners get lost in this and forget that the name of the game is to serve their clients. And it is easy to lose sight of your priorities when running a business—especially if you have not read **Chapter Two: 3 Secrets of Successful Delegation** and started delegating your to-do list.

Sometimes, there is a difference between serving your own needs and serving the needs of your clients. This can be a problem for business owners who have lost touch with their target markets. Never lose sight of what your clients need and want from you. Make sure that you fulfill a need of your target market, and not only offer what you want to provide—your business must fulfill a needed service or product; otherwise, you have just an idea and not a business.

For example, a woman I knew started a home cleaning service business in the 1980's in the Midwest. Her company provided cleaning services for homes and businesses. She loved her work and enjoyed helping people by providing a valuable timesaving service for busy people. Her business grew for the first 20 years, but started to contract after 20 years.

After some analysis, it became clear that while her cleaning services were still wanted and welcomed by the busy professionals in the affluent area she served, her inability to communicate with clients electronically meant that she was no longer meeting her clients' needs. She had to be reminded that serving her clients comes first—even if it meant she had to get out of her comfort zone and learn how to communicate electronically. In order to grow her business, she needed to stop serving her own needs at the expense of her clients' needs.

Once you stop serving your current clients, business is going to drop off rapidly. Assuming that you have gone through the exercises earlier in this book, we will now work on ways to make sure you serve your target market's needs so that they continue to do business with you and refer their friends and colleagues to you, as well.

CUSTOMER SERVICE STRATEGY 2: KNOW YOUR CLIENTS' NEEDS

If it is your priority to serve your clients, then it is critical that you know what they really want and need from you. If they don't tell you on a regular basis, how can you find out? You ask them—early and often! Think about this, how will your clients respond to your asking them how to better meet their needs? Won't they be impressed with you for asking?

Most people are happy to talk about themselves and happy to tell you what they need—*if you ask them*. Even if they are too busy to fully participate when you ask, they will still appreciate a genuine desire to really understand and meet their needs.

In our culture, we frequently say that the customer is always right, but how often is this really so? How often, as a customer, do you feel that the companies with whom you do business really understand or even know what would meet your needs? Do you believe that they care about you or your needs? What happens when you find a business that is able to communicate with you, wants to serve you and your needs better, and wants to be the best possible [fill in the blank] provider? Are you more or less inclined to do business with them? Are you more or less inclined to refer others to them?

The answer is, of course, that we prefer to do business with those companies that not only meet our needs, but also continue to strive to improve the business interaction. Now, most people do not love filling out long surveys, so I do not recommend that you conduct long or impersonal ones. In fact, larger companies have to do this, because of their size and their inability to connect in a more personal manner, but as the owner of a smaller business, you have the ability and the competitive edge over your larger competitors in this area—you can connect more personably with your clients AND in a more meaningful way.

So how do you contact your clients to ask them how you are doing and how you can meet their needs? Well, there are lots of options, but for this book, we will explore four: **telephone, in-person meetings, email,** and **online** surveys.

> **"**You have to have a way to benchmark what your expectations are for your customers and then make sure that your staff is groomed in a way that fulfills your promise of your brand."
> – Nancy Duarte Childs, Duarte Design, www.duarte.com

CUSTOMER SERVICE STRATEGY 3: THE INS AND OUTS OF SURVEYING YOUR CLIENTS

Telephone vs. In-Person Meetings vs. Email Surveys vs. Online Surveys

	PROS	CONS	OTHER CONSIDERATIONS
TELEPHONE	Clients will feel appreciated. Real-time communication allows you to be responsive right away. You have the ability to communicate directly with your clients, (re)building rapport and reminding past clients that you are able to meet their needs. Real-time connection means a more meaningful connection. This allows you to learn what they liked about doing business with you. This allows you to make changes or corrections if you learn about problems.	Some clients will not make themselves available. Some people do not like interacting on the phone. They prefer being able to respond when it works for them—sometimes after business hours. You will learn about how clients felt about doing business with you: both positive and negative.	You will need to make sure that you find a time that is convenient for your clients. Make an appointment for when it works for your client. Survey should take about 15 to 20 minutes. Longer ones are too burdensome on your clients Ask mostly open-ended questions. The best ones begin with "what" or "how". Avoid asking why questions—these can make clients feel defensive. Do not react defensively to any negative feedback. Being defensive will not help you grow your income. Listen to them, thank them, and then move onto another subject if the feedback is negative.

	PROS	CONS	OTHER CONSIDERATIONS
IN-PERSON MEETING	Clients will feel appreciated. You have the ability to communicate directly with your clients, (re)building rapport and reminding past clients that you are able to meet their needs. Real-time connection means a more meaningful connection. Asking clients how to improve your products or services is a great way to learn information, build rapport, and create a community of engaged clients. This allows you to be proactive and responsive so that you may create packages or services to meet your clients' needs. Will feel wonderful when you hear positive feedback. Information you learn will help you to market more effectively to your prospective clients.	Some clients will not make themselves available. Some people do not like getting together unless they need to. They are too busy. You will learn about how clients felt about doing business with you: both positive and negative.	You will need to make sure that you find a time that is convenient for your clients. Have a set start and an end time. Find a neutral location like a restaurant—not your office. Having a group of clients get together and ask them information on how to improve your business takes some coordination, but is very worth it. I suggest no more than 8 to 10 people at a time if you are asking survey questions. Provide food and facilitate a discussion, allowing comments to flow freely. Ask mostly open-ended questions. Best ones begin with "what" or "how." Avoid asking why questions—these can make clients feel defensive. Do not react defensively to any negative feedback. Being defensive will not help you grow your income. Listen, thank them, and then and move onto another subject if the feedback is negative.

	PROS	CONS	OTHER CONSIDERATIONS
EMAIL	Still allows you to connect, although less personal. If worded correctly, it will allow you to learn information that you can use for marketing to prospects. This allows clients to respond when they want to.	Some clients will not make themselves available. Some people do not like interacting via email. Less personal, not rapport building. Will not lead to stronger connection with your clients.	Most responses to email surveys will be short, might be only one word or two, strong possibility you will not learn much. Won't allow you to ask clarifying questions or for more information- especially if you allow for anonymous responses. Hard to get enough information for you to use effectively. You will learn some information about how clients think about doing business with you: both positive and negative.

	PROS	CONS	OTHER CONSIDERATIONS
ONLINE SURVEYS	Still allows you to connect, although much less personal. If worded correctly, will allow you to learn information that you can use for marketing to prospects. This allows clients to respond when they want to.	Some clients will not make themselves available. Some people do not like taking online surveys. Less personal, not rapport building. Will not lead to developing stronger con- nection with your clients.	Most responses to email surveys will be short, might be only one word or two, strong possibility you will not learn much. Won't allow you to ask clarifying questions or for more information- especially if you allow for anonymous responses. Hard to get enough information for you to use effectively. You will learn some information about how clients think about doing business with you: both positive and negative.

Before you chose an option, it is important to understand why you are conducting your research so that you may pick the best method for connecting with your clients, not just a tool that is easiest for you.

CUSTOMER SERVICE STRATEGY 4:
12 REASONS TO SURVEY YOUR CLIENTS

1) To find out why they do/did business with you.
2) To remind your clients that you are still in business.
3) To introduce new or improved services or products.
4) To invite clients to special events.

5) To show clients that their needs are your priority as a business.

6) To show clients that you are focused on them.

7) To show clients that you are the best possible provider/supplier.

8) To find out how to improve the quality of doing business with you.

9) To find out what went right the last time they did business with you.

10) To find out what went wrong the last time they did business with you.

11) To demonstrate your expertise as a service provider or supplier.

12) To show that you value their business and care about them as clients.

Let's break them down so you understand the goals of surveying your prospects and clients.

1) To find out why they do/did business with you. I know a number of business owners who are afraid to find out why their clients do business with them. They are afraid that by even asking, they remind their clients that there are choices. If this is you, please understand that your clients know they have choices and they have chosen to do business with you—for the moment. Asking them why is not going to suddenly remind them that they could and should be doing business with one of your competitors.

An additional benefit to learning why a client chose you as their service provider or product supplier is that you will get great information that you can use to market to prospects. Think about it, the reasons why a past client hired you will be similar to the reasons why future clients will choose you, too. Using the words of past and current clients who hired you will be more powerful to your prospects when you market to them.

Many consultants recommend that you create a value proposition or a benefit statement, which is also sometimes referred to as an elevator pitch. This is a concise statement that clearly communicates to your prospects that you know their challenges and desires and the unique contribution you and your company can provide to help them. Putting one together is very challenging, but the beginning starts with understanding why past clients chose to do business with you. You learn this by asking past and current clients why they hired you.

I recommend that you frame your questions thoughtfully. First, ask open-ended questions, rather than closed-ended ones. Open-ended questions are those questions that lead to more information being shared. Closed-ended questions lead to one-word responses, like "yes" or "no" or a number.

Second, when asking your clients questions, I suggest that you begin with "how" or "what," rather than "why." Asking "how" or "what" questions invites your clients to respond from a positive perspective. "Why" questions can make some people feel defensive, even though this is not your intention. Sample questions are included later in this chapter.

"On the advice of my business coach, Heidi Sloss, I started calling my clients and asking them specific questions about what they thought I did; what my best qualities were; what my weakness is; and who else they had considered hiring. The exercise was very uncomfortable for me, and it took a real push on my part to ask clients. Not only were the answers enlightening, they were also extremely surprising and flattering.

I was completely blown away by the information, kindness, and nuggets I received in response. Not only did I discover positive attributes about my work that I had never considered, but I also received action items I could use to improve my performance. And the most amazing part was how I could use the information my clients shared to laser focus specific advantages to potential clients.

The exercise made me realize how much a small business relies on their clients, and how effective clients can be to help a small business owner to hone their target, skills, and effectiveness.

I learned that people who have had real experience with me are a landmine of useful information to gain more clients and to improve my communications skills. I gained insight into valuable skills, many of which I had not even considered previously. It also taught me how important it is to maintain open communication with past clients, who then become not only repeat clients, but also a fantastic source of referral business. Many an old client suddenly remember they need your services, or they have a great referral when you reappear in their lives."

~ Jennifer Duchene, Lift Your Spirits Home Transformations

2) To remind your clients that you are still in business. Sometimes business owners forget to do their follow-up with past clients, and then their clients forget about doing business with them. A survey is a wonderful way to 1) keep in touch, 2) do your follow-up, and 3) remind your clients that you are still in business and still able to meet their needs.

Believe it or not, when we are not doing regular business with people, they can forget about us—this is especially true if you are not using a regular and consistent follow-up system. Meaningful engagement will keep you at the top of your clients' minds. Once you drop off their radars, they lose sight of you and your business. See Chapter Three for ideas on follow-up systems.

3) To introduce new or improved services or products: While surveying your clients about their needs, wants, and desires, you can also let them know about you and your company's latest-and-greatest offers and products.

Many times, business owners forget to let their clients know of new and improved packages, services, or products that they offer. They don't want to rock the boat, or they actually just forget. Any new ways that you can improve how your clients do business with you needs to be shared with them—early and often!

A healthcare practitioner client I had was pleased with the results she had when she called past clients to share information about her new price packages. Suddenly, past clients who had stopped coming in for services started making appointments again.

The beauty of working with past clients is that they already know, like, and trust you, so it is a much smaller hurdle for them to choose to do business with you. After all, it is much easier to convince a past client to do business with you than to get to know and build a relationship with a new client.

4) To invite clients to a special event: Holding special events for your clients is a great way to grow your business and inviting them personally is a wonderful way for them to feel appreciated and welcome. Even if they are unable to participate, just the act alone of including them is a great way to follow-up with your clients.

Holding client appreciation events is a fantastic way to grow your business. Your clients will appreciate you showing them that you are grateful and that you know they have choices. If your clients feel a connection with you, they will be more likely to continue to do business with you and refer others to do so, too.

Events can include hosting a ribbon-cutting ceremony or a client-appreciation party, putting on a special sale, introducing a new product, sponsoring a concert or sporting event, or inviting them to the theater, a picnic, or dinner. The list is endless.

5) To show your clients that their needs are your priority as a business: This is a key component of great customer service. Your clients need to know explicitly that, as a business, their needs are your priority.

What is the biggest concern we have about used car salesmen? We assume that these salesmen are only looking out after their own interests and not those of their customers. This is the opposite of what you want. You want to develop a reputation for and become known as the company that puts your clients' needs as your priority.

How do you find out your clients' needs? You ask! Call them up, invite them out, send an email, at the very least, send an online survey—although, as I have pointed out previously, you will get more traction, better responses, and better benefits if you make the connection as personal as possible. Did you know that multinational companies spend tens of millions of dollars on researching their client's needs? You don't have to spend anything to pick up the phone and talk directly to your clients.

6) To show your clients that you are focused on them: You must remember that the more your clients think you are there for them, the more inclined they will be to do business with you AND refer others to you, as well. Once your clients believe that you are no longer focused on them and their needs, they will find one of your competitors. They might blame their decision to switch providers on price issues, but the reality is that most clients leave because they no longer feel connected to you.

If you want to continue to do business with your clients, they need to know that their needs are important to you. Engaging with them through a survey will demonstrate to them that they and their needs are your focus.

7) To show your clients that you are the best possible provider/ supplier: Every time you interact with your clients, you should approach it as a job interview or sales presentation. Now, a lot of people hear sales presentation and think they must be hard hitting and convincing. This is not so. I offer a sales training program called **Seal the Deal**, in which we talk about making sure that your clients know that you are the right choice for them as their service provider or product supplier without hitting them over the head with your message.

How will your clients know you are the right choice for them if you do not let them know? How do you let them know? In all of the ways outlined in this chapter! Give your clients an excuse to engage with you and then to hire you; make sure that they know 1) how you will meet their needs, 2) that you are focused on them, and 3) that you are the best possible choice they can make.

The good news is that most of your competition is probably not engaging their clients in regular and meaningful ways. By showing your clients that you are constantly striving to improve your services and/or products, you remind your clients that you are the best choice to meet their needs.

8) To find out how to improve the quality of doing business with you: Learning how to improve your relationship with your clients is key if you want to grow your business. Take another look at the model I shared previously:

Great customer service → leads to more referrals → means more business → leads to higher prices → leads to making more $!

Being conscious of constantly improving the quality of work or service you provide will mean more money for you. Developing the reputation for wanting to improve what you offer and how you offer it is the best way to provide great customer service. People are hungry to do business with caring companies that offer a personal touch.

9) **To find out what went right the last time they did business with you:** This will help you to learn what your customers like about doing business with you, and then you can use this information in several ways: 1) as testimonials in your marketing materials, 2) to let prospects know what you have to offer, using the words of your current clients, and 3) to help boost your confidence about your goods and services. Being confident, as the expert that you are will mean that more prospects will find you appealing as a service or product provider. We all prefer to do business with experts. Experts are confident in the ways in which they present themselves. Take in the positive information that you learn from your clients and use it to boost your confidence when talking to new clients. See more about this in **Chapter 5: Why Mindset Matters.**

10) To find out what went wrong the last time they did business with you: If you are able to react positively to negative or constructive feedback, then you will be able to grow your business to new heights. Developing a reputation for being great at what you do requires asking your clients for ways you can improve. This means asking

about problems or what went wrong the last time they did business with you.

Be open to learning how to improve the quality of client interactions. This will lead your clients to want to continue to do business with you. Most people understand when things go wrong; they are willing to forgive, but only if they sincerely believe that the service provider or product supplier cares about them. Asking what went wrong the last time they did business with you is a great way to show you care. And it will help you learn how to correct problems that you might not even be aware of that are driving other clients away.

Many business owners are afraid to ask for negative feedback. They are afraid to hear what went wrong. If this is you, you will most likely lose this client anyway, so you have nothing more to lose by asking for this kind of information.

The bottom line is that you have no way to improve (and keep clients) if you do not learn about problems they are having or have had in their transactions with your company. Learning about problems gives you the opportunity to make things right, improve for the future, and keep your customers satisfied. People are forgiving IF you allow them to give you feedback and then make the situation right.

Recently, I gave a negative review of a product I bought online from a company that I have been doing business with for over 10 years. Within a week, they sent me a $50 gift card. I will continue to buy from this company, because I know that they stand behind their products. Their fast response and generous solution made me even more loyal—even though I had experienced a problem in a past transaction.

Don't be afraid to learn about mistakes, take advantage of them, and turn your mistakes into opportunities for more business.

4 Ways to Handle Negative Customer Feedback

If you receive negative feedback or comments, then I suggest you react in the following ways:

1) Thank them for the feedback.

2) Apologize for what went wrong—even if it had nothing to do with what you or your company did. If your clients have unrealistic expectations about what you can and cannot control, then it is ultimately your responsibility to educate them during the sales process. Learn from this and make sure you improve how you educate prospects and clients in the future.

3) Ask them what you can do to make the situation right. This is optional, and might not be appropriate for all situations, but if you can offer this, then do it. And be generous. If you want to cultivate loyal customers, give them something to remember.

4) Never get defensive and start explaining or justifying the situation. This will not help you in customer service and will not lead to growing your business. Since the reason you are engaging your clients at this point is to grow your business and make more money, being defensive will not accomplish either goal.

11) **To demonstrate your expertise as a service provider or supplier:** If you approach every interaction with your clients as a mini-job interview or sales presentation, you will be educating them about you, your company, and what it has to offer to them. You want your clients and prospects to know that you know their pain points, understand their challenges, and are the right expert to solve their problems. People want to hire experts (see Chapter One on the benefits

of picking a target market), and if you demonstrate your expertise, then you will have shown your clients the value in hiring you. This will also come in handy when you have a conversation with your prospects about your price points. If you have shown your clients that you are an expert, they will expect to pay what an expert charges.

12) To show that you value their business and care about them as clients: Caring companies ask for feedback. When given a choice, people prefer to do business with caring companies. Give them the "excuse" to do business with you by asking them questions that demonstrate you care about them, not just what they will pay you.

CUSTOMER SERVICE STRATEGY 5: HOW TO AVOID "DON'T ASK, DON'T TELL" CUSTOMER SERVICE

Many business owners get nervous about the idea of contacting clients and surveying them about their past business interactions. They play "don't ask, don't tell" customer service. Is this you? If so, you have a lot of company—many, if not most, of your competitors are probably providing the same style of customer service. So one of the easiest ways you can differentiate yourself and your company is to put into practice proactive, responsive customer service—become known as the company that meets their needs—something many companies talk about, but very few deliver.

In my Marketing Boot Camp Program, many business owners shared that they are afraid of being seen as needy or desperate when they ask for feedback. They think that the more they appear to be busy, the more successful they will seem. This is just not true. In fact, if you appear too busy to take care of your clients' needs, they will find another service provider/supplier who has the time to take care of them.

Once you stop asking your clients to engage with you before, during, and after their interactions with you, you will most likely lose them as a client. In reality, you have nothing to lose by contacting them, since by not asking them, you will lose their business, anyway. So if you want to keep your clients, you have to keep them satisfied. And the best way to keep them satisfied is to find out about their experience of doing business with you and your company. The best way to find that out is to connect with them directly.

CUSTOMER SERVICE STRATEGY 6: 11 QUESTIONS TO ASK YOUR PROSPECTS AND CLIENTS

I highly recommend all business owners ask their clients the following questions on a regular basis. If you have fears about asking questions like these, then I suggest you find a great business coach to help you overcome the fears that keep you from success. Mindset matters and allowing your fears to determine the outcome of your financial success is not effective. Fears can be overcome, and once on the other side, success feels great. See **Chapter 5: Why Mindset Matters** for more on this.

1) What made you select me to work as your [fill in your profession]?

2) What did you like best about working with me?

3) What did you like least?

4) What could I have done to improve my service/our working relationship?

5) How well did I keep you informed during the time we worked together?

6) What did you do when you were frustrated during the process?

7) Looking back on our working relationship, what stands out most in your mind?

8) What could I have done to make it easier to discuss problems with me?

9) What was the most disappointing thing that happened to you during our time working together?

10) Would you use me and my services again?

11) Would you recommend me and my services?

What I have been describing so far in this chapter is what I call **informal market research**, which is designed to help you improve the quality of your customer service so that you can 1) retain more clients, 2) improve your prospect-to-client conversion rate, and 3) get more referrals from past and existing clients.

Informal market research is a fast and effective way to gather market research that will give you insight into the feelings and perceptions your clients experience in doing business with you. And the information you gather will help you to market more effectively and sell more persuasively to your target market.

CUSTOMER SERVICE STRATEGY 7: INFORMAL AND FORMAL MARKET RESEARCH

12 STEPS FOR CONDUCTING INFORMAL MARKET RESEARCH

1. Call 10 to 15 past clients
2. Ask them for their help
3. Invite them to a breakfast/lunch/dinner at your expense with other past clients
4. Tell them that you want to discuss ways to improve your business
5. Time limit for about an hour
6. Works best for 8 to 12 people at a time

7. Hold event on neutral ground: hotel conference room, private room in restaurant [note: holding your informal survey in your home or office will mean your clients will feel like guests and might not really open up; honesty is what you are looking for, not a feel-good-pat-on-the-back response].

8. Start on a positive note, have the group introduce themselves, then ask each person to answer a question. Invite others to comment on what has been said—ask if they had the same experiences.

9. Ask open-ended questions. Best to use questions that start with "how" or "what." Avoid using questions that start with "why."

10. Always ask how you can improve your service, even if everyone says they were happy with your service/products.

11. Warning: Never defend or justify your actions. You want honest, candid information. Being defensive will hamper the flow of information and prevent honest answers. Justification will not increase your income.

12. Plan on conducting a session once or twice a year—this will be one of the best things you have ever done for growing your business.

If the idea of doing this in a group terrifies you, then start off doing it with individual clients and work your way into holding group informal surveys.

5 STEPS FOR CONDUCTING FORMAL MARKET RESEARCH

Want to go even further? Then I suggest you also add conducting formal market research to your business model. Here are five steps for adding formal market research to your to-do list. By the way, this is a great activity that can be delegated, as opposed to the informal market research, which is both customer service and a marketing tool.

1) Send a questionnaire to every past client in your database for the past two years. Mail the questionnaire about one week after the job is completed. [Note: what condition is your database in? Updating your database is another task that should be delegated.]

2) Your questionnaire should not be on your company letterhead. You do not want it to look like it came from you. Give your questionnaire the look of an independent research company— your clients will be more honest.

3) Include a self-addressed stamped envelope to make it easy to mail back.

4) Get a P.O. box for the return address and to be used for receiving the questionnaires.

5) Systematize sending out your formal questionnaire on a consistent basis without having to think about it.

Now that you know how your clients think and feel about the service or products you provide, you can use this information to make your sales and marketing presentations more successful—the information that you learn from your informal and formal surveys will be helpful for you to use when marketing to future clients. Want a copy of a template for a formal marketing survey? Go to: http://www.fortuneisinthefollowup.net/readers-special-gift/ and type in the password: fortune.

ACTION ITEMS:

- Start easy by contacting your favorite clients to participate in a survey.
- Put together some questions from the suggestions in this chapter.
- Ask your clients either in-person or on the phone (not via email and not via the web).

- Write down or record the responses.
- Make a commitment to conduct 10 surveys over the next two weeks.
- Take the information you learn and start using it.
  - If it is positive, tell your other clients and prospects what you learned.
  - If it is negative, use the information to improve your business.
  - Learn from what you learned.

Fortune is in the Follow-Up®:
Make sure that you always ask for referrals when surveying your clients, even if they gave you negative feedback. It might feel hard to do if they have given you negative information, but instead of focusing on the negative, figure out how to turn it into a positive situation. Ask how you can make it right. Ask what you can do to earn their referrals? If you don't ask, you won't get!

5

WHY MINDSET MATTERS

"Believe you can or believe you can't, and you will be right every time" is a version of the quote made famous by Henry Ford when he said, *"Whether you think you can or you can't, either way you are usually right."* I love this quote because it shows that how we think, feel, and talk about our businesses directly affects the success of our businesses ventures.

Mindset is not all that matters, but it is a key ingredient in my 5 POWER strategies. You could be successful and achieve your goals without a great mindset, but it would be much harder and less likely. Why wouldn't you want to do everything that you could to ensure your business success? There are many factors that affect the success of our businesses that we cannot control: market conditions, the economy, suppliers, or consumer demand. But the one aspect that we can control is our attitude or mindset.

> **"** The longer I live, the more I realize the impact of attitude on life. Attitude, to me, is more important than facts. It is more important than the past, than education, than money, than circumstance, than failures, than successes, than what other people think or say or do. It is more important than appearance, giftedness, or skill. It will make or break a company, a church, and a home.
>
> The remarkable thing is we have a choice every day regarding the attitude we will embrace for that day. We cannot change our past; we cannot change the fact that people will act in a certain way. We cannot change the inevitable. The only thing we can do is play on the one string we have, and that is our attitude. I am convinced that life is 10% what happens to me and 90% how I react to it. And so it is with you: we are in charge of our attitudes."
>
> – Charles Swindoll

CREATE A POWERFUL MINDSET

Creating a positive mindset begins with thinking positively about yourself, your abilities, and what your business has to offer to clients/customers. Let's break them down.

1.   **Think positively about yourself.**

Self-confidence is the beginning place for a positive, powerful mindset. In order to start your business, you had to come up with an idea and then have the confidence in that idea to move forward. Even if you have days in which you lose track of your self-confidence, you had to have it inside in order to make the decision to begin. This level of confidence separates the people who dream about doing something from those who actually do it.

In her book *Goal Digger: Lessons Learned from the Rich Men I Dated*, Alicia Dunams wrote about the difference between what she called Type-D and Type-DN people. Type-D are the People Who Do and Type-DN are the People Who Do Not (page 107). Many people dream of having their own business, but not everyone puts it together. Even if you are not having the success you dreamt about when you started, it took something inside yourself to decide to start your business—and that something is what you can always find inside to think positively about yourself. As you build on your successes, then start building on how you see yourself.

> **"** Believing in yourself is the first necessary step to coming even close to achieving your potential."
>
> — Sheryl Sandberg, Facebook COO commencement address to Barnard's College, May 2011

2. **Think positively about your abilities.**

Why have people chosen to work with you? Why have you been hired? Even if you do not currently have enough clients, focus on the ones you have had for the moment. Think about them and why they hired you. Start to understand that you have something of value to offer.

People do not hire you because they feel sorry for you. They hire you because of your talents and abilities. Get in touch with those talents. Take the time and write down your abilities. Keep track of what it is you can do. Keep your list nearby to remind you on days when you lose track of the ability to think positively.

3. Think positively about what your business has to offer to clients and customers.

Self-confidence sells. We are attracted to people who seem to know what they are doing and saying. How do people find this self-confidence? Are they born that way? Some are, but most have to work to figure out their talents and abilities and then remind themselves what they have to offer to people. Once you can do that on a regular basis, you can begin to translate that to thinking positively about what your business has to offer to clients and customers.

To put it bluntly, if you cannot think positively about what your business has to offer to clients, why will they? Your belief in your business will show up in how you talk to prospects and clients. They will learn what you think about your business' services and/or products by how you talk about it. So thinking positively is not a frivolous exercise. I often tell people in my sales training programs that the basis of a great sales program begins between the ears—in your mind.

> **"**Our ability to contribute to this world is directly proportional to our conviction that we have something of value to offer."
> – *This Is Not the Life I Ordered, 50 Ways to Keep your head above water when like keeps dragging you down* by Deborah Collins Stephens, Jackie Speier, Jan Yanehiro, Michealene Cristini Risley, page 68

THINKING POSITIVELY IS ABOUT KNOWING IT DOWN INTO YOUR BONES

Thinking positively is not just about thinking how terrific you are. It goes deeper than that. You have to own the belief. In other words, you have to **know** it down into your bones. This is tricky for a lot of people. They want to believe in themselves, but deep down they don't. Instead, they think negatively about themselves, and they tell themselves negative thoughts all the time.

When I explained this concept to my teenage daughter, she said, "Mom, I don't want to lie to myself." She hit the nail on this head with her comment. If you believe that you are lying to yourself when you think positively about yourself, your abilities, and what your business has to offer, then it will be lying. This lack of self-confidence problem is a deal breaker for entrepreneurs.

Business owners who constantly tell themselves negative messages about themselves and their companies are not going to succeed. Remember, if you don't believe in yourself, why should your clients? And if they don't believe in you, they won't hire you.

Beth Weisberg, Workplace Essentials, Coaching and Training for a Better Workplace, said this about believing in herself and her abilities:

"I'm all too prone to letting my inner critic convince me that I don't have what it takes for a particular gig or assignment, and I've had to learn to blast past that. Over time I've learned to say, 'Yes, I can do that'; maybe I haven't done it before, but I can do it. Maybe I have to learn something new to help me succeed on a project, but then I start becoming an expert in that, too!

I have a current project going with a public-sector client for whom I've done a fair amount of consulting, training, and coaching over the years. They approached me some time ago about taking on a big project helping them do an agency-wide training needs assessment, and I demurred because formal needs assessment is not something I consider part of my expertise. So they went off and interviewed someone else who didn't have the history with them I do. They came back to me and asked, 'Are you sure you can't do this? We'd really like to work with you on this.' So I bit the bullet and sat down with them to talk about what they needed and let them know what I thought I could—and could not—offer. In the end, they decided to work with me because they trust me and know I know them and their needs. Now I have a nice little contract with them spanning the next 6-9 months. And, of course, I'm finding that all the knowledge and experience I bring to the table is just what they need! So much for my critic telling me this is not my area of expertise! When I get out of my own way, wonderful things happen!"

When Beth stopped telling herself what she couldn't do, she was able to hear her clients telling her what they knew she had to offer. That change helped Beth remember to believe in herself, her abilities, and what her company has to offer to her clients.

Now, just thinking and believing positive things about yourself, your abilities, and what your business has to offer is not enough. Of course, you need to have the skill set to back up your beliefs, but without the beliefs, you will not get far. It starts with the belief of thinking positively.

Note: If you think you need more skills to improve what you have to offer, then go out and get more training and education. Don't masquerade a lack of belief in yourself as a need to improve your skill set. If you are not sure if you need more training, hire a business coach and get evaluated.

THE NEGATIVE MESSAGES WE TELL OURSELVES

Business and life coaches refer to the negative self-talk that people tell themselves as self-limiting beliefs. These beliefs are the things you believe and tell yourself that put you down and place limits on what you think you can do and achieve. These assumptions or beliefs you have about yourself are not based on reality, but it feels like they are. Negative self-talk is the way in which we deceive ourselves into believing that we do not have the talents and abilities that we have.

I had a client who was an insurance/financial planner come to me for help in making telephone calls to prospects. These were not cold calls; they were follow-up calls to people who had asked to be contacted by her for more information on her services. The problem was she had become unable to pick up the phone and make the calls—a critical part of her job responsibilities. She was afraid that her calls were interrupting her prospect's days. Her inability to make the calls was crippling her and making it impossible for her to do her job. She kept telling herself that her calls were an imposition to her clients. She kept telling herself this negative message over and over again, so much so that it felt real to her and she believed it.

Once she stopped seeing herself as an imposition and started viewing herself as the competent expert that she was, her inability to make the calls went away. Instead of seeing the calls as interrupting her prospect's day, she saw herself offering needed information that would help improve the financial lives of her prospects. By changing her perspective, she grew her business.

Where do these beliefs come from? For many, they are rooted in our childhood and often from well-meaning or good-intentioned parents, and other loved ones, trying to help us. Sometimes they come from teachers or other adults, trying to pass on their own limiting beliefs about their potential without even meaning to. Any negative assessment or feedback that we take as our own can become a source of limiting beliefs that can stop us from achieving our goals.

Have you ever thought or said any of these statements?

"I am not good enough."

"I will never be any good."

"I am too sensitive to be successful in business."

"I am not tough enough."

"I don't deserve success."

"I'm no good at _____."

"Others are more talented than me and have more to offer to clients."

"I am afraid of success."

"I am afraid."

"I am afraid to trust my instinct."

"It is too hard to succeed right now."

"There is something wrong with me."

"I can't see what other people see in me."

"I am always sabotaging myself."

Any statement you tell yourself that begins with, "I can't," or "I'm worthless," or "It's hopeless," or "I'm helpless" is a limiting belief that allows you to stop trying. These statements are BIG barriers to your success.

HOW A NEGATIVE MINDSET AFFECTS YOUR BUSINESS

Your mindset affects your perspective and decision-making. For example, you might avoid going after specific prospects or solving certain problems for your clients because of a negative mindset. Earlier in this chapter, Beth Weisberg didn't go after a contract that was well within her ability and talents because she forgot momentarily to believe in herself. A negative mindset will affect how you structure your business, what opportunities you see and don't see, as well as how you view what your business has to offer to clients and how it stacks up against your competition. Your negative mindset will creep into conversations you have with prospects and clients. It will show up as fears and doubts in your sales conversations—even though you do not express them directly.

NEGATIVE SELF-TALK FEELS REAL, BUT IT ISN'T

Have you ever closed your eyes and had the feeling that you were standing absolutely straight and then looked in the mirror and saw that you are tilted toward one side? Your feelings are telling you one thing, but the mirror reflects the truth. You can see whether or not you are standing straight when you open your eyes. This is also true for how your mindset can affect your perspective. If you view yourself and what you have to offer negatively, it is like standing crooked without realizing it.

I had a real estate agent client who was up for a listing to sell a prospect's home, and she knew she was competing with other agents who had more years of experience. At first, she was nervous and couldn't see what she had to offer in comparison to the other agents. After we put together a list of reasons why she should be hired, she had a whole new outlook on herself and her abilities. She stopped focusing on what she thought she was lacking and started reminding herself of the skills she had to help her clients sell their properties at a great price. When she sat down to make her listing presentation, she made what she had to offer very clear to her prospects and told them why hiring her was going to be the best decision they ever made. And she got the listing!

You perspective directly affects how you approach business opportunities. If you do not see yourself as having many possibilities, then most likely you won't.

> **"**We began to realize that if we wanted to change the situation, we first had to change ourselves. And to change ourselves effectively, we first had to change our perceptions."
>
> – Stephen Covey

SELF-TALK MATTERS

Everything starts with your self-talk. Is yours positive or negative? Can't tell? Take 15 minutes and do the following exercise.

1) Give an example of how you are good at what you do.

2) Give an example of how you demonstrate to prospects that you know what you are doing.

3) How do your clients benefit from working with you? Give an example.

4) How do clients feel after working with you? Give three examples.

5) How do you help your clients solve problems? Give three examples.

6) Outline how you help your clients. What are the problems they come to you for solving? How do you solve their problems? What do you offer that makes their lives better?

Use the answers to remind yourself of what you offer. Repeat it to yourself regularly to overcome your negative self-talk. Note: you can also use the answers in your marketing materials and sales conversations with prospects and clients.

WINNING AT BUSINESS

People often think of success as a win and failure as a loss. This perspective on winning and losing is like viewing your business success as a game. Larry Wilson, author of *Play to Win, Choosing Growth Over Fear in Work and Life,* uses the win and lose metaphor when he writes about Playing to Win versus playing the Not to Lose Game, "Playing Not to Lose is ultimately about avoiding fear."

Fear avoidance is strong in most of us, but for some, it gets carried too far and becomes their main motivation. Here are some simple questions to ask yourself to see if you are allowing fear avoidance to control your life and inform your business decisions.

EXERCISE: ARE YOU AVOIDING FEAR?

1) Do you play it safe?
2) Are you scared to take any risks?
3) Is your business strategy all about avoiding fear?
4) Do think it is unrealistic to dream big?
5) Does following your dreams seem unattainable?

If you answered yes to any of these questions, then you have been allowing your fears to control you, and it is time to make some changes. The good news is that most of your competitors are also probably playing the Not to Lose Game, too. This means you have a huge opportunity to change your "game" by changing your mindset.

THREE WAYS TO PLAY TO WIN:

1. Be comfortable with being uncomfortable. No one wants to be uncomfortable; however, when you allow your fears to drive your business decisions, strategies, and vision, you are keeping yourself from success. If you have fears, then it is time to accept them and no longer allow them to control you and how you run your business. Owning a "better-safe-than-sorry" mentality is not going to take you far.

Every time you feel afraid or feel resistance, make a commitment to stop and recognize that your fears are trying to get you to play the Not to Lose Game. I have noticed that, most of the time, fears are a wonderful wake-up call that some opportunity is knocking at your door. The question is, "Are you going to answer it or leave it outside?" I suggest that you take several deep breaths, grab the handle, and open the door to see what is outside waiting for you. The definition of an entrepreneur is one who sees problems as opportunities and can capitalize on them. This means opening the door to what is on the other side, not waiting until you are no longer afraid.

Recognize that you are not your feelings. Even though our feelings feel real to us, they are not us. Our feelings of fear do not have to define our self-worth, our value, and certainly not how we run our businesses. The next time you feel anxious or fearful, take some deep cleansing breaths and remember a time when you were not afraid. Allow these feelings to dominate. Then go back to whatever is scaring you, and notice that, right before the feeling hit you, there was a small amount of time before you started feeling afraid. This short period of time, that exists right before you start to feel afraid (or feel anything), is your reaction time. The work you need to do is to expand your reaction time so that it is longer and longer each time you start to feel afraid. This will allow you to start to separate you from your feelings of fear.

The bottom line is that you want to stop running away from your fears and instead look at your fears as a temporary reaction to problems that you can turn into opportunities.

2. Be a true entrepreneur. As I mentioned before, being an entrepreneur is about seeing problems as opportunities and then creating solutions. In order to be open to the opportunities around us, we need to be able to take calculated risks. A calculated risk is one that has been given thoughtful consideration by weighing out the potential costs and benefits.

Without calculated risk, there is no creativity or innovation in the world. Being a true entrepreneur involves accepting that sometimes you will succeed and sometimes you will fail. And, in reality, there is no such thing as a true failure IF you learn from your experiences. The true entrepreneur learns how to take their failures into consideration for their next attempt at success.

Tina Seelig in her book, *What I Wish I Knew When I was 20, A Crash Course on Making Your Place in the World,* wrote, "On the most basic level, all learning comes from failure." (Page 75)

> **"**Only those who dare to fail greatly can achieve greatly."
> – Robert F. Kennedy
>
> **"**No matter how hard you work for success, if your thought is saturated with the fear of failure, it will kill your efforts, neutralize your endeavors, and make success impossible."
> – Baudjuin

The famous story about Thomas Edison and his 1,000 unsuccessful attempts at inventing the light bulb is a great example of positive mindset. When a reporter asked, "How did it feel to fail 1,000 times?" Edison replied, "I didn't fail 1,000 times. The light bulb was an invention with 1,000 steps."

3. Dream big. Dreams are the engines of success. Without your dreams, you are just treading water. Dreams fuel our abilities to grow, take calculated risks, and find success. Playing the Game to Win is all about seizing opportunities and turning them into your dreams. What are your dreams?

A client once told me that she didn't have any dreams. She was a virtual assistant who could not imagine anything for herself or her business beyond just being able to pay her bills. Consequently, she spent much of her time without clients, and her default marketing plan was to sit around waiting for the phone to ring. Besides her self-worth and self-esteem issues, her inability to dream at all, much less big, for herself or her business meant that she was stuck playing the Not to Lose Game. No matter how much more marketing she added to her day, how much she improved her website verbiage, or how many networking events she attended, she was not going to grow beyond merely existing if she couldn't find a compelling dream to pursue. In order to turn her business around, she had to start finding something that inspired her. What she discovered was that she really didn't like working for clients she never saw in person. Working virtually for clients was sapping her ability to dream big. Once she made some changes in the structure of her business, she was able to see possibilities around her that allowed her to start thinking and dreaming big for herself.

In order to learn from your failures, start viewing them as inspiration. Here is a short list of famous entrepreneurs who all had to deal with rejection and failure long before they found success.

FAIL in Order to SUCCEED

I require my students to write a failure résumé. That is, to craft a résumé that summarizes all their biggest screw ups—personal, professional, and academic. For every failure, each student must describe what he or she learned from that experience. Just imagine the looks of surprise this assignment inspires in students who are so used to showcasing their successes. However, after they finish their résumés, they realize that viewing their experiences through the lens of failure forced them to come to terms with the mistakes they have made along the way and to extract important lessons from them. In fact, as the years go by, many former students continue to keep their failure résumé up-to-date, in parallel with their traditional résumé of successes.

A failure resume is a quick way to demonstrate that failure is an important part of our learning process, especially when you're stretching your abilities, doing things the first time, or taking risks. We hire people who have experience, not just because of their successes, but also because of their failures. Failures increase the chance that you won't make the same mistake again. Failures are also a sign that you have taken on challenges that expand your skills. In fact, many successful people believe that if you aren't failing sometimes, then you aren't taking enough risks. Additionally, it is pretty clear that the ratio of our successes and failure is pretty constant. So, if you want more successes, you are going to have to tolerate more failure along the way.

— Tina Seelig, *What I Wish I Knew When I was 20, A Crash Course on Making Your Place in the World*

1) Henry Ford failed in business multiple times before starting Ford Motor Company. And the reason the Model T is called the Model T, is that the first 19 models did not work. Models A through S were not failures, but rather were needed so that he could succeed with the Model T.

2) R.H. Macy started 7 businesses that failed before finally starting his store in New York City in 1858. Today, it is a multi-billion dollar enterprise.

3) Akio Morita, the founder of Sony, first sold rice cookers that burnt rice. He sold less than 100 of them before going on to his huge success creating an international multi-billion dollar company.

4) Soichiro Honda, the founder of Honda Motors, was turned down for a job by Toyota. He succeeded despite the opposition of the Japanese government and founded an international multi-billion dollar company.

5) Bill Gates, Microsoft co-founder, not only dropped out of college, but his first business venture, called Traf-O-Data with Paul Allen, failed before they went on to create their international multi-billion dollar company.

6) Walt Disney was fired by a newspaper as a young man for lacking imagination and good ideas. Afterward, he started several businesses that failed and left him bankrupt before founding his international multi-billion dollar success.

If you start seeing your failures as steppingstones to your success, what can you accomplish? There is a wonderful inspirational poster that says, "What would you do if you knew you could not fail?" This means that you can dream and dream big—and if your attempts at making your dreams your reality don't work at first, keep trying as they are like way stations along the path toward success.

What can a business owner do when faced with the strong likelihood that they are playing the Not to Lose Game? Remember that resiliency and success comes from the confidence you gain from learning from your mistakes and failures. In fact, failures provide wonderful opportunities to problem solve, evaluate your direction, and make better decisions for the next situation that comes our way. Without our failures, we become complacent and end up not moving forward or, even worse, being governed by our fears.

With far too many of my clients, we discover that they are using their fears as their business strategies. They are playing the Not to Lose Game. They end up thinking small, losing out and never achieving their full potential or success. If this is you, it is important to realize that you have the ability to choose something different for yourself.

ACTION ITEMS:
8 WAYS TO CREATE A POWERFUL MINDSET.

So how do you approach making changes to your mindset? How can you take the negative self-talk and turn it into positive self-talk without feeling like you are lying to yourself? Here are 8 ways to create a powerful, positive mindset for success. These Action Items are a bit longer than the previous ones, but this work is of a different nature. Take a look at them and work through the list one at a time.

1. **Commit and Plan for Positivity.** The first step is to decide you want to change to a positive mindset and then make the commitment to do so, even if you can't figure out how yet. Your desire for a better life and a better business is the beginning. They say that every journey begins with the first step, and this is true for making changes to your mindset.

There are wonderful tools, techniques, and very talented life coaches who can help. Anyone can look up resources on the Internet and start by reading how negative and limiting self-talk is damaging you and your chances of success. Understand that there are many people out in the world who do not put themselves down or question their abilities constantly. You can live your life feeling confident, excited, and successful—but it starts with your desire to have it.

Once you make the choice (and it is a choice) to change your mindset, the next step is to make a plan for how you will make the change in your thought patterns. For some, just choosing to be different is all it takes. They notice that in the act of just deciding not to be held back or crippled by themselves anymore, all sorts of wonderful opportunities open up for them.

For others, making the choice is the beginning of work that they must do on themselves in order to turn around the negative self-talk. Find a group of other entrepreneurs working on these issues and form a study group. Use this book or one of the books in the bibliography as your study guide. Read it in sections and get together to discuss the content. Use each other to help bolster your positivity.

Sometimes by just planting the seeds of the thought of changing a client's mindset from negative to positive, all sorts of wonderful opportunities start to happen. In my various marketing and sales training programs, countless business owners have made the change from negative to positive by letting go of their negative mindset and being open to embracing a positive one.

Kim Hunter of Send Out Cards, a participant in one of my programs, said a positive affirmation daily, "Thank you for the incredible and profitable day I am about to have." She reported that

❝I am a no-holds barred, don't hold a pity party kind of person, and I take that approach in everything. I believe in 'can do.' I believe in the fact that the only thing that holds me back is me. I believe in the power of attraction and the power of positive thinking. I utilize that all the time because of how important it's been for me. I believe that I set the reality in terms of that.

Another thing about my mindset that I wrote a blog about once is that I really believe in hustle. Maybe that's how I grew up, I don't know, but I firmly believe in get off your ass and make it happen. Do what you got to do to make it happen. And if you stop sitting around and waiting for the phone to ring, you'd be blown away by what can happen."

— Ann Evanston of Warrior-Preneur, www.warrior-preneur.com

starting her day with this thought in her mind helped her to plan more effectively and 'own' the idea that she can and will achieve great sales success in her business—and she did!

2. **Affirmations that work.** They may sound hokey, and that may be true, however, given how much negative self-talk some people have internalized, it will take a conscious effort to use positive affirmations to overcome them.

Basically, an affirmation is a positive statement you tell yourself that reprograms your subconscious. The idea is that you have internalized the negative self-talk and actually have been using it already as negative affirmations. These are the negative statements you tell yourself that frequently begin with, "I can't" or "I'm not." Since the negative statements have been internalized, you might not

"The Persistence Effect"

"There is an interesting phenomenon that occurs when you get serious about marketing in a focused, consistent way. You begin to get results in unexpected places. The telephone rings, and it's a prospect you spoke to three months ago saying he is suddenly interested in working with you. You go to a networking meeting that seems like a complete waste of time while you are there, and run into a hot new prospect in the elevator on your way out. You get an exciting referral from someone whose name you don't even recognize. It's almost as if the universe has noticed how hard you are working and decided to reward you.

Don't make the mistake of thinking that these out-of-the-blue opportunities are accidents. There is a direct connection between the level you put into marketing and the results you get out of it, even when it seems as if the results are completely unrelated to your efforts.

This phenomenon is so common with people who use the Get Clients Now! Program (CJ Hayden's 28-day marketing program) that it has a name: The Persistence Effect. If you persist in making 10 calls a day, every day, you will get business, but it won't all come from the calls you made. If you consistently attend one networking event per week, clients will appear, but not necessarily from the events you attended. Don't worry about why it works; just know that it works.

....It doesn't matter so much what you choose as it does that you choose. Picking 10 things you can do about marketing—and actually doing them—will break you out of the analysis paralysis, give you a plan, and get you into action. Even if you picked the "wrong" 10 actions, the Persistence Effect would make this focused activity pay off for you in some way."

– From C.J. Hayden in *Get Clients Now,* 2nd edition

even be aware that you are telling yourself these negative or self-defeating statements on a regular basis.

Affirmations are the antidote to these negative self-defeating statements. They are the positive self-talk that describes you and your life the way you want it to be or hope it to be. Affirmations are expressed as if the positive desire has already taken place. It is important that an affirmation be descriptive and use present tense and not future tense. So instead of "I want to be successful" or "I hope to be successful," the better affirmation is "I am successful."

But being too generic can mean that the affirmation is not as powerful as it can and should be. It is important that the affirmations you choose have meaning to you. Finding what others are using as affirmations is good, but creating your own is better. So even better than "I am successful" is "My abilities and talents are outstanding, and I serve my clients wonderfully."

For those who want to use affirmations, I suggest that you use words that are in your everyday vocabulary. I don't like to see affirmations using words that you don't use regularly on a daily basis.

Since you might not have the awareness of how pervasive negative self-talk might be in your subconscious, repeating an affirmation multiple times is needed for an effect to be seen or felt. I recommend that you repeat your affirmation(s) at least three times a day. And I suggest that you put your affirmations on Post-it™ paper on your bathroom mirror, car dashboard, and computer. If repeated consistently, you will find that the affirmation you start with will no longer feel as powerful as it did at the beginning. This is a good sign and indicates your subconscious is accepting the information and might be ready for a new, more powerful one.

3. Be resilient. The ability to pick yourself up and dust yourself off from rejection and failure is a must for success. Few people hit homeruns their first time at bat. Expect setbacks—don't get caught off guard by them. Know that you won't get struck by lightning and die from your failures. Learn from your mistakes. The key to resiliency is to know that you can and will recover from your failures—just like others have done.

Put together your failure resume as described by Tina Seelig earlier in this chapter. Remind yourself of what you have learned from your failures. Start to see your mistakes as steppingstones to success.

4. 30 days to better habits. As humans, we are creatures of habits and our habits feel very comfortable—even our negative habits. Since we must have habits, why not have positive ones, instead of negative ones? In general, it takes 30 days to break or end a negative habit and 30 days to start a positive one. I mean a full 30 days. Many professionals talk about 14 days or 21 days, but I have found at least 30 days to be the right time for changing habits.

Try picking one or two habits at a time that you want to either add or end. Picking too many to work on at once is overwhelming and will lead you to dropping the project before you see it through.

Make an action plan to add or end the habit you want to change. Figure out how it will work before you start. Picture it in your mind, then make the change.

Tony Robbins has a wonderful exercise that he uses to show people how picturing something before you do it will make a difference. He uses the visualization to do what he calls "Perfect Practice." It begins with seeing the results in advance in your mind,

"I have this book which is really just fantastic, and I can't remember the title of it exactly but it's something like Great Failures of the Extremely Successful or something to that effect. It is a book that chronicles over a hundred people, both past and present, who failed monumentally in something that they had attempted to do and lost millions of dollars or made fools of themselves, but then describes how they approached their failures and bounced back.

And sometimes I'll just literally pick up that book and randomly flip through a page or through a section and just read. I was flipping through it once and it was talking about how Oprah Winfrey's first station manager said to her something like, 'Oh, you are so not going to go anywhere in this television thing. You just need to hang it up.' She spent 25 years captivating the world and becoming a billionaire in that venture. Another example is Sir Richard Branson, who started his Virgin label literally because he was a virgin in business. It was his first time doing everything that he had done, but he didn't allow the fact that it was his first time to stop him. Another story that I read was about the Model T. I didn't know that the reason the Model T is named the Model T is because literally Henry Ford used every letter in the alphabet, and it was like, okay, Model A doesn't work, Model B doesn't work, Model C no, Model D doesn't work, Model F doesn't work, Model L doesn't work. And it was finally the Model T. And it kind of sounds like a cool name as if people in a think tank got together and talked about it, thought about it. But it could have ended up being the Model W."

– Sanyika Calloway Boyce of Sanyika Worldwide,
http://tvpublicitysecrets.com

with absolute certainty before moving forward. This technique has been very successful with retraining the minds of professional athletes and entrepreneurs. It all has to do with conditioning your mind to believe you can succeed. Coupling Perfect Practice with positive affirmations is a powerful way to creating a positive mindset.

5. Read inspirational books. There are tens of thousands of inspirational books available. Novels, biographies, memoirs, and how-to books all have an impact on the lives of those who read them. Find books that inspire you, that remind you of what you are striving to accomplish. Books are all about ideas and concepts. Make sure that the ideas you are reading are in alignment with your dreams, values, and visions. Readers can find new perspectives from reading a variety of types of books. How-to books are only one source of ideas and inspiration.

Don't love reading? You are not limited to reading a book these days. You can find most books on tape and, of course, there are millions of videos online that are wonderfully inspirational. I watch lectures of professors and authors whose work motivates me to think differently and approach problems with new perspectives. This makes a huge difference in how I solve problems and seize opportunities. Want some great inspiration? Look up Tina Seelig's video lectures on Stanford University's website. You are in for a real treat!

6. Listen to inspirational songs. Music that lifts you up and inspires you to Play to Win can be powerful. In some of my programs, I ask participants to pick a theme song for the work they are doing while we work together. Songs and other audio content are a powerful influence on our lives. Listening to negative or depressing music will invite a negative mindset. Listening to positive or uplifting music or an inspiring audio lecture will do just the opposite—they will invite a positive mindset. Think about what you want for the next 6 to 12 months and pick a theme song that will help remind you of the opportunities out there, just waiting for you. Pick only one theme song at a time. It is important to find a piece of music that plays to both your intellect and your emotions.

7. **Watch inspirational movies.** Visual images can be a very powerful influence on us. Like reading inspirational books or listening to inspirational music, watching inspirational movies can make a profound difference to our mindset. After her stage IV breast cancer diagnosis, Saranne Rothberg found watching humorous films to be life changing and life saving. She went on to found The Comedy Cures Foundation, www.comedycures.com, an amazing non-profit, which uses therapeutic comedy programs to help heal the sick. In remission since 1999, Rothberg was named one of Oprah's 100 most influential lives in her 2005 anthology, *Live Your Best!* She tapped into the powerful influence of visual images and humor. Bottom-line, make sure that the movies you watch are those that help you create a can-do and what-is-possible mindset.

8. **Finally, Find Your "Tribe."** No person is an island; we do not exist alone. Who we surround ourselves with affects our mindset positively or negatively. It is critical that you only allow positive people access to yourself.

We need people who are our personal cheerleaders. These are the people in our lives who remind us that we are wonderful and will achieve wonderful things. These cheerleaders are like your fan club. They are the people who believe in you and are available to remind you of your worth and value when fear and doubt creep back in. These are your people, your tribe, and their influence cannot be underestimated.

In my presentation, "Power Public Speaking for Anyone, Tips, Topics and Tactics," I talk about the importance of only interacting with positive people right before you give any presentation. In my own speaking practice, I frequently call my "tribe" and have a conversation with one of them before I get in front of an audience. They remind me of who I am and what I have to offer. This helps me to be able to be fully present and offer my presentations without negative thoughts and distractions.

You will find it much harder to create a positive mindset if your family or friends are not positive people. "Negative Nellys" are positive mindset killers. If you are unable to jettison all the negative people in yourself, you will have to find ways to mitigate their influence on you. This is not optional if you want to find success.

Add to your life whatever ways you can find to remind yourself that are you more than your fears and self-doubt. There is no reason why anyone has to remain chained to their fears and negative mindset. Reading Nelson Mandela's autobiography about his 27 years in prison, *Long Walk to Freedom: The Autobiography of Nelson Mandela*, reminds people that even under awful conditions, a positive mindset makes all the difference.

So don't imprison yourself with chains of fears, doubts, and a negative mindset. The sky is the limit with the right skill set and a positive mindset.

Fortune is in the Follow-Up®:
Start seeing your positive mindset as infectious and your negative mindset as a repellent. Someone once said, "You are what you think." If you think negatively about yourself, then when you contact your prospects, you will not have much to offer to them. If you cultivate a positive mindset, you be will able to create meaningful relationships with your prospects and clients—the foundation of all successful businesses. *"Believe you can or believe you can't, and you will be right every time!"*

INSPIRATIONAL BUSINESS STORIES

Power Strategy 5 is all about knowing what inspires you. For me personally I like to read biographies and autobiographies of successful entrepreneurs who have overcome adversity and turned their setbacks into success. In my keynote presentations I like to reference these stories and case studies as audiences find them inspirational. Here are some stories I have collected from business owners, like you, who are running their businesses in what has been called the worst economic environment since the Great Depression of the 1930's. These business people did not let the economy stop them from running their businesses, making money, and helping the economy recover. Some are small successes and some are larger, but overall they reflect a 'can-do' attitude that shows the resiliency. I hope that you find the stories motivational in your quest for business success and profitability. Feel free to send me your stories of success.

"People sometimes ask, "Why do I need a building permit?" Here is a story about a project that my company recently completed that has to do with building permits, and how following up with contacts helped to get work and revenue for my company.

I developed an ongoing relationship with a real-estate attorney who is in a same networking circle with me. After a few months of knowing him, he began giving me referrals to his clients. One of these referrals turned into a project to help a property owner legalize unpermitted construction previously done at one of her rental properties.

We went to work and after some research and a number of hours at the building department for plan submittal and permit application, we obtained all the necessary permits. Then we helped the owner complete the construction to bring the property up to code and get the various sign-offs. Her response: "Bay Area Building Permits are my angels. They have saved me from worry about what I would do to resolve this problem and everything is now legal."

I have continued to keep in touch with both this client and the attorney. It is important to my business growth to let the people know that their referrals are valued. One of the best ways I have found to do this is through making personal phone calls, thanking them, and inviting them to get together, face to face. This has kept me in the minds of people who refer me to my prospects. And I have noticed, that in this day of hands-off communication, a phone call or invitation to meet seems to be well received. I have continued to meet with this attorney and he recently gave us another referral for work.

Bottom line is that it is important to follow-up. Sometimes I worry about being thought of as pesky with too much follow-up, but if you don't keep in touch people will forget. As the cliché goes "out of sight, out of out of mind."'

Carol Graves of Abbott Lain Construction,
www.bayareabuildingpermits.com

"My business is set up with three revenue streams that include monthly clients, per-project clients, and writing clients. One of my monthly clients had to go out on emergency maternity leave for at least two months and our engagement ended abruptly. As a mom, I understood that situations like this happen, and I agreed to tie up loose ends for her and meet back up later. I quickly realized that I needed to fill this work slot as I did not want to be without that income for the time she would be off. As a virtual assistant, when my clients don't make money I can't make money! I immediately remembered some of the advice Heidi wrote about in her book *Fortune is in the Follow-Up®*, and I picked up the phone and contacted some past clients and prospects.

I am normally not very "sales-y" and tend to rely on referrals or word of mouth for business. I consider myself somewhat of a shy entrepreneur. Marketing is just not my thing. But I picked up the phone and called three past clients and three prospects that had gone cold. Within about a half an hours' time, I had several new paying clients! This was surprisingly easy. When I decided to make the calls, I pulled out my notes for each client and prospect, studied them for a few minutes, and then made the call. The conversations were so casual—it did not even feel like selling.

I knew that each person had a business concern that I could help with. Instead of saying, "Hey I'm great, I'm amazing," etc., I asked them what problems they were facing, why they felt it was an issue, and what were some things on their to-do lists that they wished they could delegate. Just touching base with each of them left behind a positive imprint of my business.

In the past, my marketing plan included several types of advertising and word of mouth. After seeing how easy it was and the great results, you better believe it now includes LOTS and LOTS of follow-up!"

Dani Magestro, Tech Admin and Writer,
www.danimagestro.com

"Out of the blue one day, I received a private message on Facebook from Rosemary (not her real name). She had been a regular reader of my fortnightly newsletter and was writing to say how much she enjoyed every issue. Rosemary wrote that she knew we would work together at some point, but for now, she had a lot going on in her life. I sent her a connection request, which she accepted, and encouraged her to keep reading my newsletters, until she decided to work with me.

Every once in a while, Rosemary and I got in touch with each other through Facebook. She shared her start-up company challenges, and I shared helpful articles and resources that I had created or come across. One day, Rosemary asked for my advice on which of my services would suit her. We discussed her situation and my support options. My honest opinion was that in her current situation, she would not fully benefit from working with me at that time. Her life was too busy, and she could not commit the necessary time

Rosemary appreciated my honesty and promised to return when things changed. We kept up the communication, through Facebook and email. I could tell she had been reading my blog posts as she sounded like a student of mine already.

Well, eventually, Rosemary did return. She bought a simple home-study course, then a long-term mentorship, and then some follow-on support. Between working together, we stayed in touch and I let Rosemary know that I was always available if she should ever need me. She kept reading my newsletters and social-media updates, so she knew about my various offers and how my business was growing. This made it easy for Rosemary to come back to me.

I strongly believe that our continued communication helped to build a bond of trust between us. Rosemary one day commented that she could see how much I really cared and it was not just about getting paid. We are still in touch, several months later and Rosemary continues to refer clients and opportunities my way."

Oma Edoja, Author, Speaker, Women's Business Growth Mentor, Oma Edoja Business Transformations, www.OmaEdoja.com

"I never assume anything about anyone and especially about prospects or clients. Having said that, I believe that when prospects don't call me back it means that there are other things going on with them personally and professionally. It does not mean that they are trying to avoid me. So until they tell me not to follow-up, I just do.

With one particular woman, who had agreed to work with me, I left several messages over the course of a month but I heard nothing back from her. I also sent her follow-up emails to let her know that her contract was ready and that all she needed to do is to sign it for us to begin working together. And once again, nothing – no response.

I did not interpret this to mean that she was ignoring me or had had a change of heart. And I did not get demanding in any way or make reference to the previous attempts I had made to reach her. Finally, I left a very heartfelt message on her cell phone, letting her know that I was not calling about business at all. I just wanted to make sure she was doing fine, and I asked her to reach out to me when she could to let me know everything was okay with her and her family for I was genuinely worried about her.

Two weeks later I received a phone call from my prospect. All I did was listen and then tell her I was glad to hear she was fine. She told me her mother had become seriously ill in another state. She had to drop everything to be with her. Her mother passed away. She shared she was so touched by my last phone message that she knew then she had made the right decision to work with me as a coach. And now that she was getting back to her life she was ready to get started with me. This ended up being a $25K contract and she has become my biggest referral partner."

Rosie "the Closer" Zepeda, Speaker, Author, Transformational Business Coach and Corporate Trainer, www.rosiezepeda.com

"A woman took my publicity course, and she could not afford to immediately do consulting. I followed up with her consistently, per her request, every 60 days. After one year, she started working with me, although not at the discounted rate I had originally offered her.

When she signed up to work with me, she told me she wanted to acknowledge my appropriate and consistent follow-up. She said that she never felt too pressured and that my follow-up was just enough—it was respectful of her requests. Consistent and persistent follow-up are key!"

Jill Lublin, Public Relations Expert, www.jilllublin.com

"During a women's networking event in 2008, I meet Nanci Worcester, a long-standing adoption attorney and the owner of Adoption Center of Northern California. She was very interested and impressed with our creative design aesthetic. I was equally impressed with her passion, dedication, and commitment to the delicate balance required in her line of business. Although she did not have an immediate need for new graphics at that time, she later contacted us, eager and ready to take her business to the next level.

As part of our follow-up system, we immediately sent Nanci our "Ezeeye intro and E|ssessment," which allows us to do both a quick overview as well as comprehensive discovery process to identify immediate, interim and long-range brand, design, and marketing needs. The E|ssessment serves as an ongoing working document to help keep all current and future objectives on track. From there, we created a full strategy and provided an outline, which was broken down into stages.

At that time, the Adoption Center of Northern California needed an overall visual brand enhancement, all new business collateral, a new website, and a marketing strategy to address the very delicate and unique needs related to her industry. We have since worked with Nancy for over three years on many aspects of not only her branding and graphic design, but also that of her entire Internet marketing campaign as well. Not long ago, it became obvious that she is ready to take her marketing to another level with mobile and app development.

Words truly cannot express the gratitude we have for Nanci's ongoing business loyalty, but more importantly for respecting our process and talent and for trusting us to develop and deliver such a vital promotional message for her safe, caring, and professional adoption facility.

We have been able to provide Nanci's business with up-to-date marketing help because we never underestimate or overlook a onetime networking connection. We are always prepared to make a significant and memorable impact and follow through with a well-developed follow-up process and follow-through system. For my business, I never make my prospects or clients have to remember me, I like to keep in touch through notes, emails, phone calls, and in-person meetings."

Deidre Trudeau, ezeeye IMAGING: Expert Brand, Graphics, Mobile App and Web Design Specialists, www.ezeeye.com

"I started my own company after having worked for someone else in the same industry for 14 years. One of my more popular items is carpet-protection film, which is installed during the construction process and protects commercial carpets from getting soiled, being exposed to debris, liquid spills—all sorts of things.

One of my customers, who I have had for about seven years, has been consistent in terms of orders. I sell job-site protection products to him – and he resells these products directly to high-end general contractors in New York City. After selling him a large quantity for him to sell to his largest and oldest customer, I learned that the product failed big time. Carpet protection film is supposed to adhere to the carpet, but in this case, not one roll out of the 30 he ordered and resold adhered. Not one. I figured I was trashed, that I had lost him as a customer and would have to let it go.

I decided to ask (in actuality I begged) my client to let me visit the job site where this took place. It is not a usual practice in my industry to allow this, but he consented – and I am glad that he did. I witnessed firsthand that the product had failed him and his client. I was beside myself wondering how I messed up in hiring this newer factory to supply my product. I asked to see the boxes that the product had come in, and it turned out that the boxes of film were to protect metal, not carpet. Metal protection film does not have as much adhesive on it as carpet film and it cannot grab the carpet fibers as easily.

Fortunately for me, I had brought a roll of my carpet film with me. It worked like a charm. I had the project manager go through the steps with me, distinguishing carpet protection film from metal protection film. He loved the exercise and thought it was cool to see the difference. I gave him a much clearer understanding of what he had bought, something my customer would not have been able to explain to him.

What happened next was incredible: He asked me if I could protect his metal ducts.

Guess what? Now, both my customer and my company, Go To Protect, have more business through that one contractor then we had before. It goes to show you that one can turn a total product failure into more success by following up and following through!"

George Larson, President, Go To Project,
www.gotoprotect.com

"What they never tell you about the wine industry.

I had to get the sale. For over a year, I had followed the process as requested. I sent samples and friendly informative sales sheets on how they would profit, and I made copious calls. My national vice president of sales flew across country to visit the company headquarters in Florida twice. They said they were interested, but the sale was not closing.

This was not just any customer I was after. It was the 4th largest alcoholic beverage distributor in the U.S. They owned the wine market in eight southern states where wine consumption was among the top in the nation. It was a critical market for our company's success and reputation as a national distributor.

Partnering with the right distribution channel partner for our product could make or break our wine business. Go with the wrong distributor and we'd run the very real risk of having wines get "lost" in warehouses while in transit or somehow placed in retail and restaurant establishments that never put them on the shelf. Find the right distributor and our wines would be handled correctly with no excessive heat or light and little vibration. Fees for having your wines placed prominently on a grocery-store shelf, miraculously evaporated. Your wines will be featured on the custom menus of top-tier restaurants, highlighting the pairing of food and wine for the high-end gourmand.

Our goal was originally to avoid distributors by going direct to consumers. I felt personally responsible to the small vintners and their families who were our providers. We began the relationships while walking vineyards or tasting in their rural home-based cool, musky-smelling, damp caves. These family growers had put their trust in us by giving us national exclusives. Exceptional Wines was a national wine importing and marketing company and touted as one of the world's first wine websites. Unfortunately, we learned through trial and error that to be successful we needed to partner with distributors in the south.

It was time to decide: should I go with our second choice or give it one more try?

I was not willing to take second best so I took action. I had done everything to get the sale except get on a plane for a face-to-face visit with the decision makers. Securing a visit to do a tasting for the top 20 executives proved to be difficult; however, my tenacity finally paid off. One day in May, 18 months later, I presented before an exalted group of wine professionals and sommeliers.

I was nervous. They were classically trained but I was not. Industry feedback was that I had a great palate. Our wines and marketing strategies were winning awards. Would they believe enough in my palate, business savvy and company to want to represent our wines to their clients?

They tasted more than 18 wines that day, listened to my stories about the wines, wine makers and regions, and looked at marketing materials and our award-winning website. In a move I would later be told was highly unusual, they selected 16 of the 18 wines tasted to add to their portfolio and they did it while I was in the room.

More than a year of following up paid off. I had secured the best distributor for our wines in the south—and we finally truly became a national marketing company."

Carol Smith, CEO, Exceptional Wines, National Marketing and Distribution Company, www.CarolSmith.com

"I credit my success on providing excellent service, but I also know that great service by itself is not enough to grow a business in a very competitive field. My thriving web development business is based on referrals from satisfied clients. Without them, I would be spending more time marketing my business than providing my clients with my services and the level of attention they deserve. In short, I would be trying to build my business, instead of actually growing my business while making money.

My referrals come from former and ongoing clients who refer me to their colleagues, friends, and lead-based groups. I know a referral by itself does not guarantee that I will get the project. That is where follow-up plays a big role in my success. I never take a potential client or job for granted.

After receiving a phone call or email from a prospect, inquiring about my services, I follow-up immediately, providing them with the information they are seeking and an offer to discuss their needs with them in greater detail. That follow-up is critical to my success, and it usually results in a telephone call during which we discuss their web development options and how I can help their business get the online presence they seek. Then I follow-up again by sending them a proposal or scope of work. In most cases, that is sufficient and the proposal is quickly signed and returned to me. On some occasions, however, I have found it necessary to follow-up several times before a client contracts my services. Even then, I know it is more beneficial to follow-up with an existing referral or former client than it is to blindly seek new clients through promotional blasts and advertising campaigns. While it might take some time and persistence, it is less time consuming and costly to follow-up than it is to start from scratch.

An additional benefit is that each time I follow-up, I am letting my clients know that I value their business. That value results in more referrals, which keeps the cycle flowing. In short, the more I value them, the more they value me. In business, you cannot put a price on that kind of value — it's worth several fortunes.

A great example of how following up works in my business involves my client, Sally, a reflexologist, whom I met at a networking event three years ago. Since our initial meeting she not only hired me to design her company's website, but she also has referred my services to several of her friends and business colleagues.

One of the several great referrals that I received from her involved her professional membership as a board member on the "Reflexology Association of California." When the board were discussing redesigning the association's web site, Sally recommended me. I was awarded the project not only because of the quality of my work but also because of the timely manner in which I followed up with the board president. Right after hearing of the referral, I presented him with a scope of work proposal and was awarded the project."

Phyllis E. Garland, CEO, San Mateo Web Design and Development, www.SanMateoWebDesign.com

"How my follow-up has grown my business:

I met my client Maggie at a decorating class I gave about seven years when I was starting my business. She signed up for my newsletter. I send out a follow-up newsletter every month with tips and information on client transformations. Through the newsletter I build trust and connection.

A year ago Maggie felt compelled to call me. Through my newsletter, I had created a sense of trust and safety for prospects. Before hiring me, many of my clients have never used services like mine. And for Maggie, by the time we started to work together, she was very comfortable because of the ongoing connection I had established through my newsletter.

I did not have to show her my credentials or proof of what I could do. She had been seeing the proof in her inbox for six years. Since the first time she hired me, Maggie has used my services three more times, each time to help her create a space she absolutely loves, which has given her the confidence to enjoy her home. A couple months ago one of Maggie's friends saw my work for Maggie, and then called me to help her with her "sacred space" and then six weeks after that her neighbor called me to do her space. So I can safely say that staying in touch and reminding people what I do, is a wonderful non-intrusive "drip" method. It may have taken seven years, but it created a solid foundation of referral-based business.

Another follow-up success story of mine is of Louisa. I met Louisa at a women's event. I was interested in her services and when I followed up to hear more, she expressed interest in mine. We ended up working for each other. And now, four years later, we are still working on projects together. Additionally, Louisa has referred me to friends and connections numerous times. She tells me how good I am at what I do, and we respect each other. Following up with her and staying in touch keeps us linked and has provided opportunities that have been both profitable and supportive.

Finally, I met Lilly at a conference where I was signing books of my newly released best-selling book Le Chic Cocoon. We were both at a party and started talking. I gave her a copy of my book. I followed up with her on Twitter. She wrote an unsolicited blog post about my book. She introduced me to other women in her circle at another conference, and told those attendees about how powerful my book was. She became an ambassador or great referral source for me. Through that introduction, I was invited to speak to a women's group that has created even more speaking engagements, book sales, great referrals, and joint venture partnerships."

Jennifer Duchene, Design Expert, Le Chic Lifestyle, www.jenduchene.com

"A few months ago, I received an email from a potential client. I was referred to this company from an existing client. We spoke on the phone and afterwards the woman I spoke with let me know they would be making a decision in the next few weeks and would contact me then. She followed up on time, but there was still no decision yet.

I thanked her for the update and took the opportunity to send a few more examples of my most recent work in PDF form.

A month went by, and I followed up with about her design needs. She responded with a fairly generic message about going with another designer, but thanking me for my time.

Normally, I would have replied "thank you" and that would have been the end of it. But instead, I decided to find out why I was not chosen. Was there something I could have done differently? Was it my location or style or price? Something else completely? I told her I always ask and would certainly appreciate any honest feedback that she could offer.

I received an immediate response, saying that it was more of the style issue that made them go with someone else; that they were looking to do something a little more funky, but she also said that she thought my work was beautiful.

I replied by thanking her for her feedback and the compliment on my work. I ended by saying that most of my work comes from referrals, so please keep me in mind if she hears of a need. And from there we connected through LinkedIn. I put her in my calendar to follow-up in three months to ask how her projects were going. But I no longer need to do that – before I could contact her, she called me and said things were not working out with the other designer. Apparently the designer became unresponsive, had some communication challenges and also seemed uninterested in the lack of creativity of this first assignment. She asked if I was still available and told me that they wanted to go with me if I had the time.

So I gained a new client all because of the art of following up!"
Wendy Wood Design, Graphic Designer, Wendy Wood Design, www.wendywood.com

"I quit my job as director of a highly successful bio-pharma company to launch a business in an industry with which I had no prior experience. Not a decision supported by everyone in my life but one that I needed to make to live life on my own terms. Now, I own a luxury goods business and I could not be happier.

During my corporate career in both employment law and learning and development, I had entire departments under my control. I had staff members reporting to me who responded in a timely manner to my requests because it was their jobs. I was accustomed to getting things done through command and control: tell them what to do — and they do it because they report to me.

In my current business, I cannot use command and control to achieve desired results. Now follow-up and relationship building are the keys to my success. They allow me to leverage myself and grow my business. I discovered that follow-up is not merely another call to a client or prospect or partner to ask them to buy a product or service. It is truly about cultivating a real relationship with people, caring about them and what goes on in their lives; spending time with them because you want to. Therefore, my follow-up activities include: attending birthday parties for their children, catching a movie together, or checking out the latest art/wine festival, etc. I show up as a human being genuinely interested in their lives, and when I do "pitch" my business, at a later date, they feel comfortable moving forward with me.

My business pitch is simple and, I think, quite appealing: Join our designer shopping club, buy original high-end jewels, handbags and more at member prices, and get a piece of all future revenues generated in the club. However not everyone says "yes" the minute they hear it. Why is this? There are a number of reasons including a genuine disinterest, issues with personal confidence, financial challenges, fear of making a decision, desire to remain in one's comfort zone, and so much more.

I recently checked my business stats and found that over 90 percent of my current clients/partners required three to four follow-ups before coming aboard. One in particular stands out. This is a woman I met at a personal development seminar and she was underutilized and insufficiently challenged in her hi-tech job. We sat next to each other and she saw my jewelry portfolio sitting on the floor. She asked if this was my business – of course this made making my pitch easy.

I went to lunch with her on the first day of the seminar, and she asked questions about what I did. I answered her questions without overwhelming her with details and certainly did not pitch to her because I wanted us to get to know each other better. She had had a bad experience with direct sales in the past and said she would never get involved in anything like that again. I told her I completely understood and listened closely to what she wanted.

She was a leader in many ways and did not feel her company recognized or rewarded this behavior. Among other things, she wanted to find a way to generate revenue that had no restrictions on her ability to advance, that allowed her dynamic personality to shine and that offered real value to customers. We talked about how her previous direct-sales experience paled in comparison to what we offered. By now, she had already seen photos of our gorgeous product and understood the value of gold, silver, diamonds, etc. And she was interested.

My plan was to follow-up with her after the event. I emailed her after our meeting to thank her for spending time with me during the seminar and invited her to lunch. She canceled the first time. Then I called to reschedule, and we grabbed dinner to celebrate her birthday, no business talk. I just wore my fabulous pieces, which she salivated over.

I followed up a week later by asking her to come by my home and learn more about the business (and make pizzas). She did, but was not yet ready to join. She had to first satisfy her doubts and do some research. When she learned we were the fastest growing fashion designer house in the world and how lucrative the business was, she began to soften her resistance. But she still did not join. So I contacted her again to meet for coffee. She canceled, called me to reschedule, and we met via phone. She asked tons of questions and finally came on board. While that may have seemed like a lot of follow-up the fact of the matter is that she is now responsible for about 50 percent of my company's production! When she tells this story, she often says that my follow-up and relationship building were instrumental in her making her final decision to join the company."

Terrace Ellis, Owner, LifeBlossoms,
www.globalwealthtrade.com/lifeblossoms

"My story shows that that luck favors those who prepare, particularly in this tough and relentlessly slow-to-recover economy.

At the end of 2008 I was laid off from Symantec/Norton Consumer Products, like so many other once high-flying technology marketing professionals. That event caused me to think about my experiences during dotcom bust of 2000/2001. At that time I was too busy climbing the corporate ladder. Taking on my first vice president of marketing responsibilities meant I had little time to pay much attention to anything else. At the time, I was not in a space where

Google and search engines had any significant impact. However, hindsight tells us, online marketing has changed the marketing landscape and skills required of a marketer forever. After absorbing that hard lesson, I decided that this time around I would "skate to where the puck is going" and became a certified social media strategist in 2009. I took online courses and, in my spare time, enhanced my knowledge by attending relevant webinars. Along the way I learned about the emergence of marketing automation software; and paid close attention to how once again, the marketing landscape was shifting with technologies like social media and marketing automation.

In March 2011, a co-founder of a marketing automation software company contacted me via LinkedIn and suggested that we meet for coffee. He was impressed by my LinkedIn credentials. That meeting led to an invitation to visit his office to learn about the LeadFormix marketing automation platform and to meet the people who created it. A month later, the same LeadFormix co-founder started referring clients to my consulting practice, for which I will be grateful forever. At the same time, he offered me the opportunity to be a LeadFormix marketing advisor and compensated me with stock options.

In January 2012, LeadFormix was purchased by CallidusCloud, an $80 million publicly-traded sales effectiveness SaaS company. By February I was offered a full-time consulting contract; and in April, I started on a permanent basis as LeadFormix's head of customer success. In July, I was elected president of the NorCal Business Marketing Association, after serving on the board as its director of social media for the past two years. My vision and goal is to lead the NorCal BMA to the Chapter of the Year award in 2013.

I feel as if I landed my dream position, after being one of the youngest graduates from the Kellogg Graduate School of Management, Northwestern University, with my MBA in marketing in 1983. After three decades of hard work and perseverance, this is where I am today: happy, contented and grateful.

If I were to sum it up, I think my success stems from pursuing a career that I love, having an action-oriented temperament, and always willing to learn new skills to keep me relevant. The chance meeting with LeadFormix's co-founder started out as just another opportunity to meet a fellow professional for coffee, but it quickly evolved into a meaningful and mutually beneficial relationship. I hope that my story will inspire people to keep "sharpening your saw," persevere and take advantage of opportunities when they present themselves. In my case, it does seem that the harder I work, the luckier I get."

Nancy Chou, Sr. Dir. of Customer Success,
www.leadformix.com

"Heidi BK Sloss' book *Fortune is in the Follow-Up*® should be a business owner's Bible to build business to succeed. If you've just got started with your business, Sloss' sage, experienced advice will inform you on what to do to follow-up properly to get business under way. If you're a seasoned entrepreneur (like I am), her words of wisdom will simply remind you about what you haven't been doing or need to do.

I recently used her advice to follow-up after a business function. I had met a woman twice at two different functions. At first, I wasn't looking at her as a prospective client (she was a fellow author), and then I thought how she could be doing more to promote her book. Rather than wait for her to initiate contact, I realized I had her business card. So, the second time I ran into her, I used Sloss' suggestion to invite her to coffee to chat. Not only did I end up having a wonderful conversation with her, I realized she needed much more assistance than I realized. I made some suggestions about how she might improve her book, and she agreed with me.

If I had not taken the initiative to follow-up, the relationship and prospective sale would have slipped through the cracks. We have these opportunities around us all of the time, you just have to follow-up and follow through to succeed. Sloss' book remind business owners to do the essential follow-up and marketing to win more business. It's a must-have book for everyone in business."

Michelle Gamble-Risley, CEO, 3L Publishing, LLC, Author,
www.3LPublishing.com

"After giving a well-received presentation a few years ago to a large group of real estate agents, I was surprised that my phone was not ringing off the hook with interested people looking to work with me. At the time my business was divided between working one-on-one with individual business owners and independent workshops that I sponsored.

My offer at the end of the presentation was timely and compelling, and yet I had not had the normal response to my presentations: more sign-ups than I can usually handle. Instead, I had a stack of business cards and not much to show for it. So, I challenged myself to make 10 calls a week from that stack of cards I had collected, to personally connect with everyone in the audience. It was nerve wracking—and I felt vulnerable, even though it had been a receptive crowd and they had responded enthusiastically. But, I had made a commitment to myself a few years ago to not let my fears get in my way. And, I had made a commitment to my family to earn a certain amount of income to provide activities and opportunities that I wanted my children to have access to.

So I took a deep breath and started on the first card. Not only was she available on the first try, but she responded that she had just been thinking about me and wanted to talk. She had an idea that became a huge success for me. Her suggestion was to take the material that I was currently presenting in my one-day sales training program for the real estate industry and turn it into a four- or five-part program that would meet every week. That way the pieces could be integrated into each business owner's business in a more reasonable timeframe. This was a great idea—and I knew that it would be a hit, but I wanted her help in setting it up. So we worked out a deal and between the two of us, we promoted it to her office and launched the first of many Seal the Deal Real Estate Learn @ Lunch programs that were a big success.

I never did make it through the whole stack of business cards that I had collected that day as each call landed me more business and great opportunities. Fact of the matter is that audience members had loved my presentation, but most of them needed a personal connection from me to help them decide to actually work with me beyond the presentation. Those phone calls more than made up for the nervousness and worry I had had before them. And I learned that the people who are my best clients are those who want a personal connection with me – like a simple phone call."

Heidi BK Sloss, Keynote Speaker & Sale Trainer,
PowerPreneur Partner, www.heidisloss.com

CONCLUSION

Small-to-medium-sized businesses are the future of our economic engine in this country. As more and more people turn toward business ownership, so will our economy grow. Chad Moutray, Chief Economist and Director of Economic Research, wrote in the U.S. Small Business Administration (SBA) Office of Advocacy's 2008 edition of *The Small Business Economy: A Report to the President,* "The 27 million small businesses in the United States play a vital role in the economic well-being of our nation."

But running a business without knowing business basics is a recipe for failure. The latest statistics state that only about half of new businesses survive the first five years. And survival is one thing, more important, businesses need to do more than just survive, they need to thrive. Business owners need to remember the basics—the sound, tried-and-true business principles that have served entrepreneurs for generations.

Business success will be a bit different for each of you. But the name of the game is: controlled growth and net profit. Is it easy? No, but adopting a back-to-basics mentality is a critical part of success; do it now and don't procrastinate. Don't get caught in the over-thinking, "analysis paralysis" that prevents business owners from moving forward. And in this shaky economy, moving forward is key. Remember, if you are not moving forward, you are moving backward.

The bottom line is to get back to business basics, don't do more activities—do the right ones that are effective. Adding more and more to your to-do list will take you further away from serving your clients, and it all starts and ends with serving your clients. "Got to keep your customers satisfied" is both a line from a great Simon and Garfunkel song AND the golden rule in business.

Why do some businesses succeed while others do not? It is not necessarily because of the superiority or inferiority of what they offered. In fact, we all know of businesses that failed even though they provided excellent goods, services, and products. And we know of businesses that don't provide anything excellent but are still around. What is the key difference? Basically it is their ability to connect, engage, and then provide to clients and customers. These successful businesses do not necessarily have more capital or larger marketing budgets, but they are committed to business basics: marketing essentials and sales strategies that make a difference. And the great news is that you can commit, too!

More is not more when it comes to knowing business basics and then following them. You aren't dependent upon external factors like the economy. As a business owner, you are dependent only upon your commitment to the POWER strategies as outlined in this book. It isn't rocket science, but it takes focus, effort, and commitment. As I said previously, not all businesses will make it; however, those that succeed are those that choose to follow the 5 POWER strategies with energy, focus, and passion. There are few short cuts, but the road to success is well paved and well lit. Stay on the path, listen to your clients, and then dedicate yourself to earning their business. This is the way to growth, success, and earning more money!

BIBLIOGRAPHY

BOOKS:

Babauta, Leo. *The Power of Less.* New York: Hyperion of HarperCollins. 2009

Collins, Jim. *Good to Great.* New York: HarperCollins, 2001

Conner, Marcia L. *Learn More Now: 10 Simple Steps to Learning Better, Smarter, and Faster.* Hoboken, New Jersey: John Wiley & Sons. 2004

Covey, Stephen R. *The 7 Habits of Highly Effective People, Powerful Lessons in Personal Change.* New York: Simon & Schuster, 2004.

Covey, Stephen R. *The 8th Habit: From Effectiveness to Greatness.* New York: Simon & Schuster, 2004.

Duarte, Nancy. *Resonate, Present Visual Stories that Transform Audiences.* Hoboken, New Jersey: John Wiley & Sons. 2010

Dunams, Alicia. *Goal Digger: Lessons Learned From the Rich Men I Dated.* San Francisco: Bush Street Press. 2007

Hayden, C.J. *Get Clients Now!(TM): A 28-Day Marketing*

Program for Professionals, Consultants, and Coaches. 2nd ed. New York: AMACON. 2007

Levinson, Jay Conrad, and Al Lautenslager. *Guerrilla Marketing in 30 Days.* 2nd ed. Jere L. Calmes of Entrepreneur Press. 2009

Reis Al, and Jack Trout. *Positioning: The Battle for Your Mind.* New York: McGraw Hill. 2000

Stephens, Deborah Collins, Jackie Speier, Michealene Cristini Risley, Jan Yanehiro. *This is Not the Life I Ordered, 50 Ways to Keep You Head Above Water When Life Keeps Dragging You Down.* San Francisco: Conari Press, 2009

Schwerdtfeger, Patrick. *Marketing Shortcuts for the Self-Employed.* Hoboken, New Jersey: John Wiley & Sons. 2011

Seelig, Tina. *What I Wish I Knew When I Was 20: A Crash Course on Making Your Place in the World.* New York: HarperCollins Publishers. 2009

Stanny, Barbara. *Overcoming Underearning: A 5 Step Plan to a Richer Life.* New York: HarperCollins. 2007

Stanny, Barbara. *Secrets of Six-Figure Women: Surprising Strategies to Up Your Earnings and Change Your Life.* New York: HarperCollins. 2004

Wilson, Larry, and Hersch Wilson, *Play To Win! Choosing Growth over Fear in Work and Life.* Austin, TX: Bard Press. 1998

Wiseman, Richard. *The Luck Factor, Changing Your Luck, Changing You Life: The Four Essential Principles.* New York: Hyperion. 2003

U.S. Small Business Administration (SBA) Office of Advocacy's 2008 edition of *The Small Business Economy: A Report to the President.*

LECTURES:

Brazile, Donna. Keynote to Professional BusinessWomen of California Conference (PBWC). 10 May. 2011.

Kawasaki, Guy. "The Art of Innovation." Mountain View High School. 4 Feb. 2010.

Sandberg, Sheryl. Keynote to Professional BusinessWomen of California Conference (PBWC). 10 May. 2011.

Seelig, Tina. "The Art of Teaching Entrepreneurship & Innovation." Stanford University, Stanford Technology Ventures program. 27 May. 2009.

Seelig, Tina. "Levers for Unlocking Creativity." Stanford University. 26 April. 2011.

Speier, Jackie. Keynote to Professional BusinessWomen of California Conference (PBWC). 10 May. 2011.

Woodruff, Lee. Keynote to Professional BusinessWomen of California Conference (PBWC). 10 May. 2011.

ACKNOWLEDGEMENTS

Over the years, I have been told by a variety of people that I should write a book. While I fully expected to write a book one day, I never expected to have one done this year. Basically, this book was written in a weekend and then refined over the next four months. I could not have done it without the encouragement, support, and gentle nudging from my publisher and book coach, Alicia Dunams. Thank you.

Others who have encouraged me professionally as a writer, speaker, and business mentor include Marcia Conner, Helene Van Manen, Sanyika Calloway Boyce, Phyllis Garland, Julie Shanson, Patrick Schwerdtfeger, and Jay Conrad Levinson. Your encouragements, ideas, and support nurtured me when I needed it.

Additional thanks to the five industry leaders who agreed to be interviewed for my book, Jay Conrad Levinson, Ann Evanston, Nancy Duarte, Sanyika Calloway Boyce, and Alicia Dunams. I learned much from your insightful responses to my questions.

A special thank you to my online scrabble buddies—thanks

for the great distraction to help me get through the writing, Jeanne Townsend and Pat Booth.

Of course, without the love, support and, most of all, belief from my husband, David, this book would not be possible. Watching you write your books is inspiring. We have known each other for 33 years and been married for 22 of them. Thank you for continuing to be my life partner.

And finally I want to acknowledge my clients from my businesses over the years, going all the way back to 1980. Thank you for trusting me to be your keynote speaker, your business mentor, your trusted advisor, your product supplier, and your service provider. Each of you has touched me, and I have taken what I learned from working with and for you and turned it into this book.

2nd Edition Acknowledgements

This past year has been a whirlwind, since the first edition was released to great success. Lots of my success is due to the help of several key people. Danielle Magestro, my assistant and right hand, has been an integral member of my success team. Peter Winick, strategist extraordinaire, helped me to see the big picture. And a special shout out to Michelle Gamble-Risley of 3L Publishing, who I met years ago at an eWomen event and who really knows how to nurture a relationship. Thank you for believing in me and this book. Your work on the 2nd edition was invaluable. I am thrilled to be joining your stable of talented authors at 3L.

ABOUT
HEIDI BK SLOSS

Heidi BK Sloss teaches independent sales agents and business owners how to think, breathe, and behave more entrepreneurially. She's given over 200 keynote speeches, sales and leadership trainings, and break-out presentations to groups as intimate as 20 and as large as 2,500. Her specialty is working with teams of Real Estate, Mortgage, Interior Design and General Contractor professionals on the key sales strategies and proven client attraction techniques that she honed as an independent sales agent with Coldwell Banker, where she was a top producing sales agent year after year.

After working with Heidi, her clients regularly experience double-digit increases in their close rates, overcome the paralyzing fear of selling, and learn how to attract all the clients they can handle.

Heidi has been an entrepreneur all her life, her 31-year history spans from building a direct sales business from the ground up, to running an international manufacturing firm, to playing an active role in the success of a global non-profit. She knows firsthand what it means to be an independent sales agent and how to overcome the hurdles, common obstacles, and daunting roadblocks that can keep independent sales professionals from reaching their full potential. Now, with the release of her book, *Fortune is in the Follow-Up®*, she is helping even more entrepreneurs and independent sales agents connect with their inner salesperson. Visit her online at www.HeidiSloss.com.